Winners Never Quit

WINNERS NEVER QUIT

HOW TO BECOME A COURAGEOUS LEADER

MARKUS BOHI

NEW YORK

LONDON • NASHVILLE • MELBOURNE • VANCOUVER

Winners Never Quit

How to Become a Courageous Leader

Published in New York, New York, by Morgan James Publishing. Morgan James is a trademark of Morgan James, LLC. www.MorganJamesPublishing.com

Proudly distributed by Publishers Group West®

Morgan James BOGO™

A **FREE** ebook edition is available for you or a friend with the purchase of this print book.

CLEARLY SIGN YOUR NAME ABOVE

Instructions to claim your free ebook edition:
1. Visit MorganJamesBOGO.com
2. Sign your name CLEARLY in the space above
3. Complete the form and submit a photo of this entire page
4. You or your friend can download the ebook to your preferred device

ISBN 9781636984216 paperback
ISBN 9781636984223 ebook
Library of Congress Control Number: 2024931008

Cover & Interior Design by:
Christopher Kirk
www.GFSstudio.com

Morgan James is a proud partner of Habitat for Humanity Peninsula and Greater Williamsburg. Partners in building since 2006.

Get involved today! Visit: www.morgan-james-publishing.com/giving-back

DEDICATION

This book is dedicated to my incredible family.

My wife, Sandy, has been instrumental in my growth and perseverance through life's challenges. I'm so grateful to have you by my side through life's ups and downs. I love how your heart is so big, and it shows in everything you do -- from your continuous support and guidance of our kids and grandkids to the way you volunteer in the community.

My kids -- Stephanie, Erik, Joel and Mitchel. Each of you is such a vibrant and accomplished individual, and I know your impact on this world will be strong. To say I'm proud is an understatement.

My parents, Hans U. and Doris, are the backbone of my character. Growing up, you both instilled values and morals in my heart and mind that carried me far in life. I miss my mom dearly, and I'm thankful for my dad and our regular conversations about all things business and current affairs.

My brother and sisters – Kaspar, Susanna and Barbara. Each of you stood by my side since I was a child. From our days playing outside together to living across the globe and starting our own families, our bond never wilted. Thank you for your relentless support throughout all these years. I miss Susanna's creativity and open mind immensely. But I know that she and my mom are shining down on our families each and every day, and for that I am grateful.

BOOK DESCRIPTION

There's a distinct formula that separates winners from losers. In today's competitive world, it's becoming harder and harder to win. The leaders who embrace the formula are the ones who take their organization to the top. Those who don't continue to run on the hamster wheel trying to figure out why they're not moving. So, what's the formula? What do Tim Cook and Sheryl Sandberg know that others don't?

It's simple: they've mastered the secrets to unlocking their executive power.

In *Winners Never Quit*, author Markus Bohi shares the ten elements that have led to not only his success in building and selling various, multi-million dollar companies, but the success of other leaders he has consulted in doing the same thing. These best practices have helven hundreds of leaders step into their power and, in turn, increase revenue, innovate product lines, and establish themselves as industry leaders.

If you're ready to take your career to the next level, this book is for you. It's time to learn the secrets of the winners and start creating a legacy.

TABLE OF CONTENTS

FOREWORD

I never saw snowboarding as a job. Snowboarding was simply what I loved to do.

From my teenage years that passion continued to grow and consumed my mind day in and day out. By pushing the boundaries of what was possible on a snowboard, it gave me the opportunity to travel the world making lifelong memories with friends that became my family, The Forum 8.

This came with a need to treat my passion on a professional level. The business side of snowboarding was new to me. I was overwhelmed by all the details involved in negotiating sponsor contracts, especially with company owners. I worried that most owners only saw me as a dollar sign and nothing more.

Then along came Markus.

He changed my mind.

His smile was truly genuine, he was genuine. Instead of making me feel like a commodity, he made me feel like I was being welcomed into his family. Markus cared about my opinions, listened to my ideas, and most importantly he believed in me.

Markus believed in his visions and turned them into reality. He knew what it was going to take to make something truly special in the snowboarding world. I'm proud to call Markus my friend and truly enjoyed our time working together.

Chris Dufficy

Message from the Author:
THE POWER OF BELIEF

We all come from different backgrounds.

Each unique experience we've lived through has molded us into the people we are in this moment. Those experiences should not be underestimated, not even the little things. Rather, they likely hold the key to what it takes for us to win as leaders. When we look back at the building blocks of our upbringing, it becomes apparent that the compounded experiences of our lives have built our mindset.

Our perspective toward life, business, and relationships stands on the shoulders of the experiences we have lived through up to this point and the learnings we pulled from each of those experiences. Those learnings define the level at which we drive toward new heights. The level at which we create, lead and empower. Those learnings help define our level of belief in both ourselves and the forces around us that guide our success. When we believe in ourselves, we will go far. But when we believe in something greater than ourselves, anything is possible.

When we believe in ourselves, we will go far.

But, when we believe in something greater than ourselves, anything is possible.

That very thought is what has gotten me through the constant push and pull of life over the years – whether it be personally or professionally. My upbringing and life learnings are visible in the successes and failures I've seen over the years. From my faith to the times when perseverance was the only option, I can pinpoint how each element of my life has played into the mindset I embody today.

I was fortunate to be raised by parents who wanted to give their children a balance between structure and freedom. While I learned a lot from my dad and cherished every moment spent with him, he was often away traveling for work. That didn't stop me from learning from him. One of the most important lessons I've learned was to be honest, fair and correct, and I learned it from my dad. In turn, my mom had her hands full trying to keep my three siblings and I on the right track. She did an amazing job balancing the approach between structure and freedom, and I can say that the precise combination of that was what allowed me to learn responsibility and respect. It served me well in life, and it's something that I'm very grateful for. From her, I learned to be supportive, generous and have a good heart; the importance of family and family meals together, how to treat everyone fairly and equally, support and spend time with the elderlies, among many other important things.

I grew up in Switzerland for the first 20 years of my life, and my upbringing was far from boring. Not only was I allowed to wander by myself as a child – I would even bike 30 kilometers away from home to get to my aunt's or to my grandparent's lake house. I worked and made my own pocket money at a young age, whether it was helping my aunt with the garden or cleaning the chicken coop, working on the family farm, or in the forest.

Our small town had a population of roughly 1,800, and there were only two churches – a Protestant church that my family belonged to and a Catholic church. These were the two predominant belief systems in that area at the time. My education was heavily influenced by my family's religious beliefs. My middle school curriculum included taking Bible study with the Pastor and attending church as a requirement. At the end of the ninth school year, when we completed all our bible studies and services, we were cleared for Confirmation.

I also spent many years with our town's Boy Scouts. Different than in other places, such as the United States, Switzerland's Boy Scouts don't have parents involved. Our only companions were one or two leaders who were usually not much older than the Boy Scouts themselves. This meant that we would all have to contribute during camp. We'd have to comply with what was needed from us and work together to keep things moving. We had a sense of ownership in all that we did, and we knew each of us played a role in the success of our camp. This instilled in me a sense of responsibility and respect that helped me later in life when it was time to do my mandatory service with the Army.

The Army expanded my realization of responsibility and respect. Between drills and sergeants shouting orders, I walked away with a newfound sense of discipline. I learned the true meaning of authority, and I became aligned with what it meant to lead and follow.

In 1979, it was time for me to venture outside of my shell. My friend Alfred and I left home with one goal – to spend about one year traveling around the United States and Canada on a low-budget adventure. From Switzerland, we took a train to Brussels where we got a cheap Capitol Air ticket to JFK — the Big Apple. Once we landed, we got into a taxi to take us from the airport to Manhattan. The man charged us $100 for the commute fresh off the heels of an immigration officer crushing our hopes of staying a year in the States solely due to the amount of money we had in our pockets. We were devastated by this bad experience (a hundred dollars back in 79 was a lot of money, particularly for us) that we only spent one night in NYC and took the Greyhound bus to Washington DC the following morning where we could stay with family friends in McLean.

"A year?" the immigration officer asked. "I give you 5 months, and that's *if* you manage your money well." That left a bittersweet taste in our mouths to start the trip. We were happy to be there but that lurking doubt hovered over us as we settled in. Regardless, that didn't stop us from making the most of it.

While in McLean, we spent a couple of afternoons looking for a car. We narrowed it down to a Ford Bronco and a '69 Chevy Impala. We chose the Impala because of its huge trunk — a perfect place to store all our belongings. The rest of the days down there were spent sightseeing in Washington DC. One week into our stay, I began to get very sick. I called a friend of my parents, Kay, to explain the pain. Kay used to be a nurse and lived nearby in Scarsdale, NY. Based on our conversation, she diagnosed my pain over the phone as a problem with my appendix, and she asked us to drive up to Scarsdale promptly.

We drove up to Scarsdale, just outside of New York, the next morning. Kay already organized my visit to the hospital in advance and as soon as we arrived, she took me to the hospital in White Plains. Kay's diagnosis was correct and the doctor confirmed that my appendix was about to burst, and I required surgery immediately. That was just a drill for what was about to come a few years later.

The rest of the travels took us up the East Coast into Canada, where we stayed on a farm belonging to a family friend of Alfred's. We worked for room and board, and we were also able to gain experience in our profession. When we weren't with friends or relatives, we always spent the nights in our tent to save money. If the campground did not have showers, we would, at times, stop at remote motels along the highways and check for unlocked rooms that had not yet been cleaned to grab a quick shower. We did what we had to do.

The next stop was Eau Claire Wisconsin, where we worked for a few weeks on a dairy farm. Those folks liked ice cream so much that they bought it in 5-gallon buckets. Needless to say, we had ice cream every day. While we were at the dairy farm, we were also able to prepare our Chevy for the long trip up to Alaska. We knew that about 1,500 kilometers were still gravel road and a lot of trucks were driving on the Alaska Highway so we figured it would be in our best interest to protect our radiator and headlights from rocks. So, we took matters into our own hands and welded a metal frame with small but heavy-duty chicken fencing on the bumper. That's right, chicken fencing. We also bought a couple of used wheels with tires since we knew there were no repair shops along the way.

I returned to the United States in 1982 to earn a bachelor degree in Operations Management from Cal Poly Pomona and an MBA from the University of Southern California. That's when I met my future wife and her two kids, Stephanie and Erik. During my studies, I was quite busy. I had to take many undergraduate courses that did not transfer from Switzerland, so I took many classes each semester to finish quickly. After all, I was in this country with a student visa and not allowed to work. Even so, we still had time to go on dates and travel together. We got married in the summer of 1986 in Switzerland, and our first son Joel was born in the Spring of 1987. Seven and a half months after Joel was born, with another baby on the way, we celebrated Thanksgiving with family.

My aunt Kathrin and uncle Ruedi, from Switzerland, were vacationing in San Diego and joined us to celebrate Thanksgiving. Since my uncle was a doctor at the Inselspital in Bern, my wife asked him about a bump she detected on my neck. It had been a topic that was on our minds for some time. That Thanksgiving, he felt the bump and without hesitation, he told me I needed to have it removed and checked. The very next day, I called my local doctor who made time for me within one hour. His opinion was the same as my uncle's, and he immediately sent me to the hospital where they performed a biopsy. My wife waited for me in the waiting room of the hospital during the biopsy. I was still under anesthesia when the doctor came out to talk to her.

"Hello, we're done with the biopsy. The operation went well, but unfortunately, the lump is cancerous," the doctor said in a deep, concerned voice.

"You must be talking to the wrong person," my wife told the doctor, "I'm Mrs. Bohi."

"No, ma'am. I am talking about Mr. Bohi. He has cancer," the doctor replied.

I was diagnosed with Hodgkin's Disease, a type of cancer that attacks the lymphatic system. My faith and belief were truly tested at that moment. Everything else I had gone through up to that point was made to be minuscule. How could this have happened? Even with the innate fear and worry that overcame me once I heard the news, the sobering thought of cancer lit something within me that balanced the doubt. I was determined to beat it, and I wanted to prove to myself that there were bigger things at play. A higher power was in charge and in control of everything, and I continued to remind myself that it was to His will, not mine, that everything would be okay.

With the help, support and strength of my wife, we built our tool belt to get me through it. I armed it with everything that would help me *believe* that I would emerge triumphant from the challenge. It required not only belief in myself, but belief in what was greater than myself. I walked into health food stores asking for advice, I read countless books on the topic, I received counseling from a psychologist throughout the period of treatments, who helped me deal with my emotions and the feeling of uncertainty, and who taught me mental imagery. I still use mental imagery to deal with stress, migraine headaches, challenges, etc. And lastly and most importantly, I anchored my eyes on the Bible, on my family and on our unborn child. Mitchel was born in early August and my last chemotherapy treatment was around my birthday in October.

I needed to believe. With all these tools, and after ten months of chemotherapy, I was cancer free. The disease never came back. Like the examples of authority, responsibility and mental imagery mentioned earlier in this chapter, you will see that many lessons we learn early on in our lives are being applied throughout the life as time goes on, again and again. The moral compass that guides me today is grounded in the experiences I've gone through and the challenges that defined my mindset. The beliefs and learnings I was exposed to as a child and the obstacles I overcame later in life were paired together like fine wine and aged cheese. My faith was instilled in me at a young age, and it's where I found the strength to persevere through my first solo journey to the states and even beat cancer.

My discipline was instilled in me in my youth through my time in entrepreneurial ventures, in the Boy Scouts and the Army, and it played a role in helping me build multiple, multi-million dollar enterprises and lead organizations to new heights in their endeavors toward big business. Every experience, large and small, had a profound impact on my life. Both the things I chose and the things I didn't choose shaped me in ways that I may not even realize. Regardless of the challenge, everything always worked out. I owe that to the power of belief.

There is no power quite like belief. When we believe, it becomes easier to find the strength and courage to take what has been given to us and turn it into something amazing. As we lead our families, friends, teams, and our greater organization to new heights, we would benefit from embracing each element of ourselves. Dissecting the learnings of our upbringing, exploring the lessons from our biggest setbacks – looking back on these things is like mining for gold. That gold is what will keep us from quitting. It will keep us in the light as we flip the pages of this book to truly discover what it is that sets us apart from others.

A *good* leader finds new ideas and guides people in manifesting those ideas; a *great* leader embraces their unique learnings throughout life to empower their journey, their decisions, and their innovations. The source is different. Dr. Peter F. Drucker once said that management is all about doing things right, while leadership is all about doing the right thing. To be a winner in your field, you should never quit when the going gets tough. You shouldn't take your foot off the gas. Rather, you have to give it to God. When you believe in something bigger than yourself, you will *do* something bigger than yourself.

Chapter 1
BE A PIONEER

The businesses that win, I mean truly win, are those that are pioneers.

It's the companies and the visionaries that create and innovate a product, service, or industry to new heights. It's the organizations and brilliant minds that find new ways of doing things and disrupt the mundane. But, how do these companies get to a state of being innovators and pioneers?

It's a formula. The formula comes down to what we've discussed thus far, and what we will discuss in the coming chapters. However, it inherently comes down to three things: belief, passion and tenacity.

When you are passionate about something, it shows, and people will be drawn to that passion. Now, being a pioneer?

That takes more than just passion. It takes grit, determination, and a whole lot of courage. It's hard, and that's why there are so few who pave new paths for society to walk on. Those who do it know that it's worth every drop of sweat and tears. It's worth it not only because you get to carve out *your own* path, but because you forge new relationships along the way. You get to make a real impact in the world, and that is something that we all should aspire to do.

> **Being a pioneer takes grit, determination, and a whole lot of courage. But it is so worth it.**
>
> **Not only because you get to carve out your own path, but you forge new relationships and make a real impact in the world.**
>
> **And that is something that we all should aspire to do.**

We spoke a lot in the last chapter about the power of belief. We must marry that very belief with our passion and tenacity. This formula is what fuels the engines of the pioneers of the world. Your *belief* in the work *you are tenaciously and passionately pursuing* is non-negotiable. You must believe in yourself and your idea if you want others to believe in it too. The more passionate and tenacious you are in your pursuit, the stronger your belief will inevitably become. More importantly, this same mindset needs to be instilled in your team. It needs to be ingrained in your company culture, and all sails need to be moving in the same direction with the same force.

When I was in 7th grade, I came up with my first business idea: selling rabbit fur. None of my friends were thinking of ways to innovate, let alone make money by being their own boss. That didn't stop me. I became the first entrepreneur in my class.

I was smart enough to know I shouldn't waste resources or money if I really wanted a decent return on investment. Knowing that, I asked my aunt for permission to use her chicken coop to breed my rabbits, Franz and Berta. Chickens and rabbits, as I learned, could easily coexist, and the coop provided a safe environment for all, especially as we needed to watch out for foxes and other hunters. It was a win-win situation.

After Franz and Berta had their babies, I partnered with a neighbor who agreed to help me kill the rabbits and clean the skin. He would keep the meat for himself and to sell and hand me the skin on a stretched wooden frame that helped make it nice and dry. Once it was ready, I would sell the fur. I was sure my product was great, but to my surprise, my rabbit fur quickly came in higher demand than I thought. Since each fur was a different color, people would use them to decorate their beds or as a carpet on the floor. Some would even incorporate fur in apparel items.

That successful business experience helped me understand something that would benefit me for the rest of my life as a businessman and a leader: *You must surround yourself with the right people.* When you are a pioneer, you will meet many naysayers. Many people will tell you your idea won't work, there will be skeptics and pessimists. Don't let them phase you. Don't let them get to you or derail your vision for what is possible. I was also fortunate to have supporting parents.

Who you surround yourself with in your personal life will reflect the heights you will reach professionally. Seek out like-minded individuals who support your dreams and who will help you bring your ideas to life. These are the people who will become your biggest cheerleaders and help you achieve things that you never thought possible.

This is precisely the mindset that pushed my wife and I to go for everything when it came time to give our retail pharmacy business a boost. We worked together, both harnessing a supportive mindset toward helping each other achieve our goals. At the time, we owned two renowned drugstores in California — Larson's Pharmacy & More in Colton and Moreno Valley Drugs in Moreno Valley. A few years later, we bought Model Pharmacy in Folsom and renamed it Model Pharmacy & More.

After some time in the business, we knew it was time to modernize our processes if we wanted to continue being successful. After a fruitful time of research and due diligence, I started working with the information services and systems giant, National Data Corporation (NDC), based out of Atlanta. My interest and knowledge were such that in 1987 when they started working on a pharmacy automation system, they invited me to become part of their Advisory Board. The idea was to be able to invoice insurance companies and the government electronically instead of printing out billing information and snail mailing it to each of them on a weekly basis. Mind you, this was in the '80s. We were using 2400 bps modems, which were extremely slow, but it still worked as we envisioned it.

Through their own innovative products, NDC helped us become pioneers in the independent pharmacy arena. In 1988, when NDC developed their cash register system with barcode scanning capabilities, our two stores became the first independent drugstores west of the Mississippi River to have a point of sale system (POS) in use. Other large retailers such as grocery stores were already using similar systems, but we paved the way for other independent retail drugstores and pharmacies that carried big front-end inventories such as ours. At that time, during advisory board meetings, we already talked about electronic shelf tags. We are talking about 35 years ago. We envisioned initiating a price change of a product in your store, all you had to do is access the computer in the back office and change the price. It would then show the updated price on the electronic shelf tag and scan the product at the cash register with the updated price. It was a genius idea.

As with anything new, the transition was a challenge. We were in uncharted territory. We were making it up as we went. We took a couple roads that led to a dead end before we arrived at our desired destination.

This brings me to another key element that comes with being a pioneer. You must be prepared to work hard and persevere, *regardless of the roadblocks*. Even when you think you've hit a wall, you need to dig deep until you find a way to the other side. Being a pioneer and leading a team toward new endeavors means that you will have to put in the hours. There will be late nights and early mornings. There will be times when you want to give up, but you must remember that you are working on something bigger than you.

It is only you that holds an idea in your mind the way that you do. That idea is unique to you, and it could be the very thing that your company needs, your industry needs, and even the world needs. You see, when we get an idea, it's *always* worth exploring if it's aligned and in tune with the greater strategies and objectives at play. Do not let your inspiration sit unattended. It could be the very thing that pushes your organization to the top.

So long as you know and expect times to get hard, you will be fine. No matter what you do, it will be hard. Pick your hard. It's up to you to push through those challenges and allow it to shape the end result as it will. Nine times out of ten, those challenges along the way will have only made the end result even better. More importantly, it will make you stronger and more equipped once you reach your destination. Just remember *why* you started down this path in the first place and let that drive you forward.

I may have been a pioneer in several instances in my life, but I have been surrounded by pioneers as well. I am thinking of the professional snowboard and skate athletes who were part of our action sports brands. They are pioneers — no question! Remember, they are professional athletes so they are one in a million. They invent new tricks on snowboards and skateboards, they practice and practice and practice, they fall, they crash, they get hurt, but they always stand back up and start over until they get it the way they envision it. The trick, the jump, ... They don't give up, they don't quit - they are WINNERS! I was very fortunate and honored to be part of their lives and careers.

Being a pioneer isn't just about being first. Never let that single factor blind you. Being a pioneer is about blazing trails and championing new ideas. It's about having the courage to do things differently, even when others say it can't be done. It's about having a destination in mind and mapping out a path to get there, regardless of the lack of visibility of the path we need to take to arrive there.

As a pioneer, your vision needs to be stronger than your roadblocks. Your purpose and belief need to be stronger than your challenges. Your tenacity and passion need to be stronger than your upsets. With that, your wins will be stronger than your losses. If you slow down or stop when the road is blocked, you're quitting. Quitters never win. Dust yourself off, pull yourself up by your bootstraps, and keep moving forward.

Chapter 2
MAKE 3-STEP DECISIONS

As an entrepreneur or business leader, you are constantly making decisions that will impact your business.

Some of these decisions seem easy and small while others feel like they can make or break your success. Regardless of the importance and complexity of each decision you make, one thing will always be true: *you can't afford to rush into anything.*

The truth of business is that the smallest decisions compound into a big impact over time, whether we realize it or not. Whether it is deciding where to open up another location for your organization or what you plan to do for this year's annual client appreciation event, we should always take our time in visualizing the outcome we want before we pull the plug on a decision.

This isn't always easy.

There are a lot of factors to consider and often not enough information to base our decision on. That complexity makes it vital to have a clear understanding of our goals, how much risk we can handle, what our long-term plans are, and how we can get there. If we want to disrupt industries and shake the status quo, the trail to get there is hidden. It has yet to be discovered. It is our job to discover it. The only way to discover the correct trail is to become crystal clear on the destination. Take time to dial in on the future state of your business in three, five, or even ten years. The more vivid this vision, the better decisions we will make, so long as our decisions are not rash.

To help me keep my feet on the ground through decisions big and small, I follow a 3-step process on how to keep a business going in the right direction. This process has proven useful during all my endeavors and has helped many of my clients in their pursuits as well. If you begin implementing this into your day-to-day decision-making process, you will minimize your mistakes and optimize your progress.

3-Step Decisions

Step 1: Due Diligence

The first step to take before making any decision, big or small, is *due diligence*. Do your proper research. What case studies are available to you that illustrate a similar situation you are in? The beauty of this day and age is that any question or curiosity can be answered by a quick Google search. Don't waste that gift.

If you're deciding on something as big as finding the next best location, then go visit the site. If it's finding a new manufacturing plant, ask for data on production, capacity, quality control, costing, production lead times and more and compare them to others through a diligent RFP process. If it's something small like figuring out the best client appreciation events, then Google the most effective client appreciation tactics and see what you find.

Step 2: Consult Ideas With An Expert

The key is being resourceful. Once you have that foundational knowledge and a better ballpark you want to play in, the next step is to *consult your ideas with other experts*. The fact of the matter is that unless you have made decisions on the same matter multiple times before, then you don't know what you don't know. Lean on people who do know. Nobody in the world is successful without the help and guidance of others. Lean into that and you'll make stronger, wiser decisions.

Step 3: Consider All Outcomes

Once you've dialed in on a shortlist of different directions you could go, then *consider all the possible outcomes* that will come with each choice. For example, if you are selecting a new ERP system, you will need to understand the strengths and weaknesses of each of the systems on your shortlist. Consider how your team will adopt the technology, the risks associated with the investment, and how your processes will change as a result of the new technology. If you are down to three event venues, then play out how each event would feel at each venue. No matter the scale of the decision, you need to live with the outcome for a moment and evaluate the good and the bad that will come with the decision.

Sure, this will add some time to the overall decision-making process. You may think that you have no time to waste and need to be quick. But, you would be surprised by how taking enough time to make an informed decision makes a difference. Think about it. When you make the wrong decision, it haunts you. The remnants linger and seep into other elements of the business, ultimately pushing you off track. What's worse? Falling off track or taking an extra day or two to make sure you are making the right choice?

When I started my rabbit breeding business in my younger days, I didn't have much to lose. Even so, I didn't just go for it out of a hunch. I made sure to ask around amongst my potential customers, and solicited input from experts. In this case, I asked adults (since I was still just a kid). I asked the man who later became my partner, who had farming experience and a clearer understanding of the risk-benefit correlation. The information I gathered helped me determine there was in fact demand for both rabbit meat and fur. Only then did I go for the exciting part of setting up shop, promoting my business, and offering my friends, family members, neighbors and other customers an innovative product.

Your peers, mentors, advisers, and customers (current and prospective ones, equally) will always have valuable insights and unique perspectives that you may not have considered. These insights are vital to understanding where you're standing and where you need to head next. See what they think about your ideas and get their feedback on potential courses of action. After all, if you start a business and there aren't enough people interested in that product or service, it will have no value. Even if it's an amazing idea, you will lose a lot of time and money.

Far too often, clients come to me with an incredible idea. They start on the process of turning that idea into a reality, but somewhere along the way, they wonder what the next best step is. Taking the next correct step requires that you use both your intuition and experience. It also requires a high level of awareness of your business or industry environment so you can react appropriately as things come up.

Take as an example my two retail pharmacies in California. Both drugstores were high-cost of goods and low-profit margin businesses. After doing market research and considering our client's needs and expectations, we determined that for the stores to succeed and be more profitable, we needed to modernize them – making improvements from inventory to logistics and technology. So, not only did we automate the purchase and billing process to make it more efficient, but we also made changes to our front-end store. This was in the 80s, but like many 21st-century independent drugstores, you could find over-the-counter products, cosmetics, greeting cards, and all kinds of household items in our pharmacies. It was a great offering, we just needed to work smarter and make things easier for our clients.

This was also the time in history when computerized cash register systems hit the market, we invested in the new technology and instead of receiving the merchandise and labeling it manually each day, we started using the barcodes that already came with the products to scan the products. Apart from the logistics and time management benefits this had, we could now easily handle price changes or inventory management tasks more effectively by using this system. More importantly, it helped us with a security and loss prevention issue. We had to deceive clients who would come in and remove a low-price sticker from a product to put it on a higher priced product with the intent to pay less at the register. It happened a lot, and was resulting in us losing money. That system helped us stop it.

However, it took courage, belief and tenacity paired with the 3-Step Decision process to take the leap and invest in technology when nobody else was doing it. Decision-making can easily turn tricky if you're not careful. You may seek the input of experts, potential clients and other people, and later on, overestimate or underestimate the value of that information.

Then again, we're human, and we each have our own set of interests, values and biases. But, in business, you'll never do anything bigger than yourself if you only see what you wish to see and hear what you wish to hear. Take the time to evaluate your options and understand the information in your hands so you can make more accurate decisions.

> **"**
>
> **We are human, and we each have our own set of interests, values and biases.**
>
> **But, in business, you'll never do anything bigger than yourself if you only see what you wish to see and hear what you wish to hear.**
> **"**

A recent client of mine at Bohi Consulting experienced the power of the 3-Step Decision firsthand as they started to scale their company. They were in the snack bar business and were struggling to get the brand off the ground. The challenge was centered around the fact that this was a specialized snack bar, which makes it different from other major classes of bars such as granola bars, protein bars or meal-replacement bars.

Our job was to help this client by gathering market research, identifying trends, and helping them make other decisions that would fill in their business plan. Through the process, we identified that while their target customer base was excited about this product and ready to get it from the shelves, the manufacturing process initially laid out was not the correct one. Their bar needed to be manufactured as an *organic* product if they wanted to make any substantial sales. The data from our market research showed that their target customer wasn't as intrigued by the snack bar if it was to remain a regular snack bar.

Now, this was a new product that had not been launched yet, so there was $0 in sales. Making hundreds of boxes of each flavor of a perishable item to only test its luck on the market was not the safest and smartest thing to do. This is where evaluating our options and understanding the information came in. We were able to identify a factory overseas that was able to manufacture the bars in small batches, allowing us to make samples, test them, and then produce them in larger quantities once we were sure about the quality and sale potential of the product.

In this scenario, the client took the time to study the research we completed and presented, consulted us for guidance, and they thought through whether the product was ready to hit the shelves. This is just one example of how taking the next correct step is a competency that must be developed through practice, experience, patience, and awareness of your business. I know that few things in life are as exhilarating as starting your own business and that there's nothing quite like the feeling of taking a bold idea and turning it into a reality. But, running a business is not all fun and games. Making tough decisions is an essential part of being a successful entrepreneur, and it's often one of the most challenging parts of the job.

> **❝**
> In business, knowing how to take the next correct step is a competency that must be developed through practice, experience, patience and awareness of your business environment.
>

Yes, trust your instincts when making decisions for your business. But, you must also take your time and think things through carefully before taking action. The process is all about having a vision, managing risks, and finding ways to get to the right solutions to make it happen. It doesn't mean that you'll always make the right call, after all, we're all human and can make mistakes. However, with some careful objective planning and thoughtfulness, you can find feasible solutions to your challenges, make the best out of your money and time, and ensure that you're always moving your organization in the right direction.

Chapter 3
CONFRONT CHALLENGES HEAD-ON

I f you're not prepared to face challenges head-on, you'll never succeed in life or in business. This is one of the most important pieces of advice I can give to any entrepreneur, executive, colleague, or friend. It's something that I live by every day. We are all constantly confronted with challenges, whether it's in our personal or professional lives. How we deal with those challenges sets us apart. It determines whether we will win or lose.

It's easier said than done. Oftentimes we run into situations that put us between a rock and a hard place. Maybe it's a matter of our industry evolving, requiring us to decide how we want to pivot. Maybe it's a matter of addressing personal or professional relationships that have gone sour. Maybe it's confronting a cancer diagnosis head on. Whatever the challenge is, you will always end up stronger on the other side if you embrace the challenge completely. Welcome it, dance with it. If you run from it, it will chase you and linger over other aspects of your life until it's addressed.

When I think about this concept, I can't help but to remember the biggest challenges I've faced during my career. Most of them came during my years in the action sports industry. While it was one of the most stressful stages of my life, it was also the one that brought me some of the best experiences I live to tell.

In 1995, when we started our Forum Snowboard brand, we began manufacturing snowboards in a factory in San Diego. Forum snowboards were ridden by professional snowboarders who used our gear in competitions. We had countless customers and sponsored athletes counting on us to deliver a strong, great quality gear that performed well so they could perform well. There was little room for error when it came to production.

Not even three months into production, things went into disarray. All my positivity, patience, focus and determination were suddenly tested one morning as I got a call from our production manager.

"I'm at the factory and there's no one here. Doors are locked, there are no cars in the parking lot, and all the lights are out," he said nervously.

"Let me call the owner," I replied.

I called and I called again—couldn't get a hold of the owner. All my efforts to locate him and mitigate the situation he had put us in failed. As I placed the calls that went to voice-mail - for the tenth time, my stomach dropped. Everything we had worked so hard for was suddenly in jeopardy. We needed to find a new factory, and fast. My biggest worries were:

- We had agreements in place with professional athletes which included monthly minimum payments plus royalties.
- We had a whole group of employees dedicated to the Forum brand, from design, development and testing to marketing, sales, logistics and back office.
- With Special Blend and Foursquare already quite successful brands in the industry, many people (competitors) were watching us and sometimes, it felt, just waiting for us to fail.
- Our reputation was on the line.
- Our employees and our athletes relied on us to put food on their tables and roofs over their heads, not to mention their families as well.

I immediately reached out to my network of confidants to discuss the urgent need of a new snowboard factory. The closest factory we found that met the requirements to produce our product was in Quebec, Canada and it was quickly reaching its capacity limit. We couldn't waste time to start the negotiations, so within twenty-four hours, my production manager and I were jumping on a red-eye flight to Quebec.

After long meetings with the factory team, we agreed to work together and give our best to finish our production quickly. They agreed to help us maintain the high-quality we had aimed for from the start.

In situations like this is when quick but cold thinking becomes important. The moment I realized the owner of the initial manufacturing plant abandoned the ship, I knew I had to take action immediately. We couldn't afford a stop in production, and although we had agreements in place and were already invested in that location, I couldn't wait to see how things would play out. So I jumped in. I moved toward a new way of doing things, and I was careful as I did it. Those quick and mindful actions required all of my courage, determination, positivity and strength I could find in myself. If I stayed stagnant, it would have simply wasted time.

I knew that, even if the owner called me back in deep apology, they were not the right fit for us. If we had waited any longer and invested more time in exploring and moving factories and warehouses, we would have lost significant business and caused a much larger disruption in our production line. Our business would have faltered. But, it didn't. In fact, we grew the brand so big that we were later acquired by Burton. I'd call that a win, and no challenge big or small was able to stop us.

The same feelings and concerns resurfaced many more times in my life but two of the most impactful were when our footwear factory chose a non-approved toe box material for our limited edition, early launch Muska Pro Model shoes in late 1999. This problem could not be easily fixed and we had to replace some shoes because that material broke. The next was when the snowboard boot factory had to send teams with sewing machines and materials to our warehouses in California, Canada and Europe and correct a construction problem on some of our snowboard boot models. Keep in mind, in each of these cases, it affected the amount of product sold which in turn affected the compensation to the pro athlete as well as the sales and profitability of our company.

We were tested, and we learned something from it. We realized that if you use your mental and emotional strength to push through when things get tough, you can turn your challenges into exciting opportunities and experiences. You can make lemonade out of lemons. When you get good at thinking on your feet and having that wit in uncomfortable situations to keep the ball rolling in the right direction, you will get closer to the finish line.

> When you use your mental and emotional strength to push through when things get tough, you can turn your challenges into exciting opportunities and experiences.

Be **intentional** about thinking on your feet. When you harness the skill of thinking on your feet and develop a sense of resilience, there are few things in the world that can knock you down. Sure you may fall off track in scenarios, you may have to take detours. But so long as you stay focused and motivated, you will develop the stamina to keep going even when it feels like you've hit a wall.

It takes courage to face your challenges head on. What is courage? It's not the absence of fear—it's taking action despite our fears. Instead of wallowing in pessimism or playing the victim, have compassion for yourself and the situations you find yourself in. Challenges are an opportunity to learn and grow, so embrace them with positive energy and a sense of adventure.

Confronting and overcoming challenges head-on also requires a dose of confidence and faith. Everyone has different beliefs, and you have to find what works for you. For me, I always turn to God to ask for strength, courage and guidance. When things feel out of my control, I give it to God. It settles my mind, and I find a new sense of power and purpose each time I give my burdens to a higher purpose. It's through that practice that I have found myself persevere and rise above any challenge that has been thrown my way—professionally and personally.

You must believe in yourself and your ability to solve whatever problem is in front of you. This inner belief helps you build up your confidence by allowing you to focus on setting goals and taking consistent action towards them. There is one caveat—don't allow yourself to become overconfident. Know your strengths and weaknesses, and seek help or guidance when appropriate. When faced with a challenge, you need balance in order to make the right, mindful decision. After all, how can good things find you if you always let your emotions take over and cloud your judgment?

The key is to look at the situation objectively, and remove an emotionally-rooted reaction from the equation. Weigh the positives and negatives, play out the end result of each decision in your mind before you take action. You must be level headed and think clearly about the situation and what needs to be done in order to make the right decision. Refer back to the 3-Step Decision making process when in doubt.

The last thing I will leave you with when it comes to confronting challenges is to never, ever give up. It's not an option. This isn't just something that applies to us entrepreneurs or business leaders—it's something that everyone should live by. No matter which avenue you choose to go down, there will be challenges.

So long as your purpose and vision are stronger than the obstacle, you will never quit.

Chapter 4
CHOOSE LEADERSHIP CAREFULLY

Culture eats strategy for breakfast — *Another pillar of leadership stated by the great Peter F. Drucker.*

The people you surround yourself with will have a profound impact on your ability to weather the storms of life. They will also play a monumental role in your capability and belief level when it comes to your goals and dreams. When you set out to achieve great things, it's important to remember that you can't do it alone. A strong team is the foundation of any successful organization, and choosing wisely when assembling that team is essential. But, how can you identify the people who will truly be an asset to the team?

During my time as a Boy Scout, I learned about the value of leadership and the importance of having the right people in those leadership positions. We were a small troop of around twenty-five scouts, and we had just one primary leader and two sub-level leaders. I had the honor of obtaining a sub-level leadership role once I was a teenager. This experience taught me many things about leadership at a young age.

There are two types of leaders, no matter the country, industry, organization or mission at hand:

1. **The ones who take the charge and have initiative.**
2. **The ones who are innately followers but want the leadership title.**

Anyone can be a leader, but it takes a special kind of person to be a **great** leader. Great leaders are the ones who take charge and go above and beyond, not just for themselves, but for the good of their team or organization. They inspire others to be their best and work together towards a common goal. They are also the ones who are willing to accept responsibility when things go wrong and learn from their mistakes. Now those who want the title but not the responsibilities are probably just looking for a way to pad their resume; they're uninterested in doing the hard work required to lead a team to success.

I'm a perfectionist at heart. I want to see things get done well and on time. I have always tried my best to lead with initiative, drive, and motivation. This has allowed me to attract like-minded people who share my same values and who are willing to work hand-in-hand with me on common goals. The keyword here is *attract*. When you are vocal and strong in your stance and show unwavering commitment to your own values, people with similar values will be drawn to you. Mirror your company values and your personal values as best you can as an owner, and if you're in a leadership role, then only serve the organizations who have similar values to your own. Only then will there be true synergy.

This is especially important in business, having the wrong people on your team can turn troubling very quickly. Negative attitudes and behaviors in a team can spread like wildfire, damaging morale, and causing everyone to question their commitment to the organization. It starts to show in the team's productivity, effort, and quality of work. Over time, this will inevitably seep into the general performance of your business and the satisfaction of your clients. It's one piece of the domino, and it can cause the rest of the pieces to fall when not attended to.

But how can you tell if someone is going to be a good fit for your business? Of course, there's no foolproof method, but there are certain characteristics that tend to indicate success. Here are the key attributes you should look for during the hiring process.

KEY ATTRIBUTES TO LOOK FOR WHEN HIRING

People who are proactive

—

Good communicators

—

Independent workers

—

People with good attitudes

—

People with applicable or transferable skills

—

People with experience

Notice the common theme in the list above—the list leans more heavily toward soft skills. If you have the most brilliant person in the world sitting in front of you at the hiring table, it will seem like a no-brainer that you should hire them. But, what if they are rude? What if they're not a team player? What if their values aren't genuinely aligned with your company values? Consider a different candidate.

That's right. Look elsewhere. Assuming the candidate has the foundational knowledge to do the job, hire a candidate based on whether or not they are the right culture fit. That is the key to creating a synergistic team. Technical skills can be taught to anyone who is willing to learn them. However, the willingness to learn is not so easily taught.

Hire for soft skills. Now, no matter the role, there needs to be an understanding of the processes and tactics at play. But so long as that basic knowledge is there, your hiring decision needs to lean toward the soft skills of a candidate rather than the more technical skills.

> **❝**
>
> **Technical skills can be taught to anyone who is willing to learn them.**
>
> **However, the willingless to learn is not so easily taught. Hire for soft skills.** **❞**

There's an old saying that rings true—a team is only as strong as its weakest link. The right people will have the right behavior, and this can be contagious, inspiring others to uphold the company's values and culture. The opposite is true as well. The wrong people will have the wrong behavior, and this can be contagious, discouraging others to uphold the company's values and culture. Don't underestimate the power of your company culture and how your hiring decisions can mold and shape that culture, for better or for worse.

In addition to finding the right culture fit, it's important to understand holes in the current team's skillset. When building your team, you must also remember that you're not the best at everything. This may seem like a simple concept, but it's one that can be easy to forget in the heat of competition. Hiring people with different skill sets and people more skilled than me has only made me better. Why? Because they challenge me and push me to be better.

I'm constantly learning and growing as a person. I've been in both small teams and large organizations with a team spread across several countries, all with different cultures, languages, and values. Taking the time to shape that diverse team by learning to communicate carefully and effectively, respecting each other's differences, and understanding how to best complement each other helped me make our businesses more well-rounded and successful in the long run. The key is to embrace both your unique skill set and your limitations and use it to build a strong team of talented individuals who can complement you. To do that, you need to humble yourself. If you're unsure about it, make a list of things that drain your energy when you have to do it. Outline the tasks that you often drop the ball on or simply don't like doing, and find someone who enjoys doing those things.

This is something that my sons learned from me and have been able to use as they shape their own career. In fact, we've been in a constant cycle of learning from each other since they were kids. Every year, starting at the age of two, we would do multiple ski trips together. Teaching the boys how to ski was so much fun! Then they grew and got hooked on snowboarding. Of course, they wanted to ride a Forum board. They enjoyed it so much that they decided to teach me how to snowboard, and our family trips turned into snowboarding adventures. It has also served them well as professionals. I love watching my son Mitchel build his company, The Forum Group, and assemble his team.

I'm certain that on top of his skills and own experiences, he has been able to use lessons he has learned from me and my businesses, especially when it comes to carefully selecting each person he will add to the team. He is also always prepared to help and teach his team members as long as they have the right attitude, commitment and moral compass, and that's something I value very much as a businessman, and as his father.

Whether you're starting a new team or have one already in place, step back and think of this: your team is the foundation of your organization. The stronger and more cohesive that team is, the better you'll be able to weather any storm. Even if you're the smartest person in the room, you won't be able to accomplish much if you're surrounded by the wrong people. Look for people who are smart, positive, and driven. Look for people who inspire you to be your best self and help you achieve the visions you've set forth for your company. Invest in those people, and they will invest in you. That's the power of a strong team.

Invest in your team, and they will invest in you. Because that team is the foundation of your organization.

The stronger and cohesive that team is, the better you'll be able to weather any storm.

Chapter 5
BE A LEADER OF THE PEOPLE, NOT THE BRAND

People over profits. It's all they talk about in graduate school.

However, the reality is that once leaders jump off the ledge of their ivory tower, *people over profits* becomes a saying that is clouded by the countless responsibilities that sit on an executive's shoulders. You think to yourself —

- *I need to make my investors happy.*
- *I need to maximize bonuses this year.*
- *I need to keep from going out of business.*

As a leader, you have a lot on your shoulders. Not only are you responsible for production and performance, but you also have countless people depending on the profits of your company. From shareholders to partners to employees to suppliers and customers - and always not only the individual, but rather their entire families. If you think about it, they're all depending on the company's profits, right?

If you want to be a truly great leader, it comes down to putting your team first. Winning isn't about getting ahead at all costs. It's about enlisting the help of others to achieve a common goal. When you put your team first, they'll be more likely to return the favor. In turn, they'll put your company first because they'll know that you're working for the good of the team, not just for yourself or for the people at the top. They'll trust you and believe in you, and they'll be willing to go above and beyond to help your company succeed.

In fact, I once had a partner who put himself in front of the team, and the team quickly abandoned my partner when the going got tough.

When I was recruiting employees for our drugstores in California by the late '80s, there was no such thing as a benefits package – those that today include health insurance, a 401k, paid time off, etc. Actually, it wasn't until after 1959[1], when Congress created a program of health benefits for federal employees and labor unions began to demand better benefit

---

1   Social Security History | Special Collections | Chronology https://www.ssa. gov/history/1950.html#:~:text=September%2028%2C%201959%20The%20 President,Federal%20Government%20and%20the%20employees.

packages for their members. Even though it wasn't popular or widespread, my team and I were determined to support our employees in any way we could. We wanted to take care of them. Slowly but surely, we began to roll out new benefits, new perks, and new add-ins that would sweeten the pot for the employees that held up our business.

In the mid 2000's when the gasoline prices really spiked, we did something simple that made a big difference. We split our team into two groups and assigned times every month when one group would take a workday to work from home, usually a Friday. The reason for this perk was the savings it created by not driving to work a couple days a month. On those days, the other group covered the bases. Mind you, remote work was not an option at that time. All the technology that allows us to transfer calls or use computer systems across different devices was not available in those years. But, it didn't matter.

Taking extra time off not only helped our employees save money on gas and meals, but it also meant they no longer needed to choose between participating in their kid's events or going to medical appointments and working to earn their money. We would even give them payment advancements if they had an emergency to help them feel secure and supported.

You don't have to do what others do, you don't have to wait until others take the initiative to show their employees they care. If you care, then show it. You can also show it in other, possibly even more effective ways. An article by Forbes discussed a study about the connection between employee engagement and wellness[2] from an important and valid perspective: engagement and wellness are an integral part of business strategy, not a task that your human resources team will barely get to scratch the surface. An engaged and healthy workforce can have a major impact on a company's success. Happy, engaged employees are more productive, more likely to stay at their company, and can even generate a substantial competitive advantage in their industry. This goes beyond offering perks like gyms or catered lunches - true engagement and wellness strategies address the physical, emotional, and mental health needs of employees, and also offer opportunities for development and growth to foster a sense of purpose and fulfillment in the workplace. Why? Because, as the article points out, "employee engagement consists of concrete behavior, not an abstract feeling."

In today's competitive business landscape, it's no longer enough to simply focus on profit margins, we must show that the company values their employees' overall well-being. As a business leader, it's important to remember that your employees are not just cogs in a machine, but individuals with unique experiences and perspectives. Showing that you care about them means fostering a positive work environment where they feel valued and respected. The study discusses that one way

---

2   Forbes | 10 Timely Statistics About The Connection Between Employee Engagement And Wellness | Naz Beheshti |https://www.forbes.com/sites/ nazbeheshti/2019/01/16/10-timely-statistics-about-the-connection-between- employee-engagement-and-wellness/?sh=204a50622a03

to do this is through peer feedback and recognition based on company values. This not only helps improve collaboration and performance, but also shows that every employee's contributions are valuable.

Inclusiveness and diversity also play an important role - by ensuring a diverse range of perspectives are represented and heard, employees feel more comfortable bringing their authentic selves to work and individual differences are celebrated rather than stigmatized. It's crucial to lead by example through empathy and respect. Empowering your employees and listening to their thoughts and opinions will not only improve morale, but also drive innovation and success for the entire organization because they will feel connected to their work and the overall mission of the organization. Just take this statistic as motivation: "disengaged employees cost U.S. companies up to $550 billion a year." Let that sink in.

Of course, leading a team comes with many challenges. You can be the most incredible leader and still come across certain people who will take it for granted and spoil the pot. One of the most difficult aspects of leading people is dealing with dishonesty. Whether it's an employee who steals funds or takes credit for someone else's work, an employee who sabotages their teammates' efforts to appear better, or someone who embezzles money from the company, dishonesty is cancerous. It cuts down the company culture, it makes others feel unheard and unappreciated, and it diminishes synergy across teams.

These kinds of incidents can be incredibly damaging to your business and painful for you as a person. However, while it may be tempting to give into feelings of anger and frustration in such situations, it is essential that you resist those urges and instead use them as learning opportunities. By reflecting on what went wrong and empowering yourself and your employees to think critically about the situation, you can develop stronger communication skills and become more resilient when faced with adversity.

Another important thing is that as a leader of people, you must be adaptable. Change is a constant in the business world, and what your employees need and expect from you can change over time as well. It's up to you to keep up. That might mean changing your management style, adjusting your company's policies, or even offering new benefits.

Take the recent trends as an example. We're seeing more employees demanding to have the opportunity to work remotely, work part-time, or prioritize having time off over receiving monetary incentives. It is also essential that you understand and embrace the unique cultural backgrounds of your team. I used to live in Switzerland, where taking time off to rest and recharge is an important part of work culture. In fact, after having worked at the same company for several years, one can earn 4, 5 or 6 weeks vacation and most folks collect all of it every year. In the United States, I've learned that it's culturally more common to skip days off. I worked with one manager for many years that I had to ask to take a vacation.

Even if you don't have a presence in multiple countries, it is very likely that your team will be composed of diverse people. It's critical to be intentional about understanding your employees on a deeper level and accommodating as best you can rather than forcing a square peg into a round hole. Sooner or later, the peg will break.

One evening I received a phone call from our office manager in Hong Kong. She told me that she does not appreciate to be "yelled" at and would have to find another job if this continued. I asked her who yelled at her. She told me but I could not believe this person from our US office would yell at her. I talked to her a little more and found out that she received an email from the US office which was all capitalized. I learned that capitalized writing in Hong Kong and China means yelling.

Diversity and inclusion are a business imperative rather than a nice-to-have. By staying in tune with the needs of your people, you will be better able to meet the needs of your employees. This, in turn, helps to foster higher levels of engagement and productivity in the workplace. In fact, studies show that highly engaged teams show 21% greater profitability[3]. This is because diversity and inclusion bring

---

3   Forbes | 10 Timely Statistics About The Connection Between Employee Engagement And Wellness | Naz Beheshti |https://www.forbes.com/sites/

a wealth of unique perspectives and ideas to the table. It enables companies to tap into a wider talent pool, creating opportunities for individuals from all backgrounds to thrive in their careers. Additionally, it fosters a positive workplace culture that highly values that individuality as a complement to collaboration, leading to higher levels of job satisfaction and employee retention. Diverse teams are often better at innovation and problem solving. They also have the ability to better understand, relate to, and serve a broader range of people, leading to a wider customer base and even the ability to outperform competitors and generate higher profits.

Ultimately, we help our business grow when we take the weight of stress, anxiety and uncertainty off our employees shoulders and "acknowledge, respect, and treat everyone equally irrespective of their identities[4]". But this goes beyond just hiring a certain percentage of minorities or setting quotas for certain demographics. A diverse workforce also brings a variety of skills, perspectives, and experiences, which can lead to better team collaboration and to more innovative and creative ways of achieving your business goals.

---

nazbeheshti/2019/01/16/10-timely-statistics-about-the-connection-between-employee-engagement-and-wellness/?sh=204a50622a03

4   Importance Of Diversity And Inclusion For Business Growth | Entrepreneur | Anjan Pathak https://www.entrepreneur.com/en-in/news-and-trends/importance-of-diversity-and-inclusion-for-business-growth/384828#:~:text=A%20diverse%20and%20inclusive%20workplace,society%20and%20higher%20employee%20retention

Furthermore, understanding different cultural viewpoints can help you become a more effective communicator, enabling you to reach out across teams and build strong relationships with people from all walks of life. As a good leader, it is up to you to understand what your team needs in order to help them succeed and thrive both individually and as a part of the greater organization.

This is something my son Joel learned firsthand recently. He's been managing marketing efforts for a hospitality brand for five years. Then suddenly, he received a significantly higher paying job offer from a company in a completely different industry.

"What do I do?" he asked me.

"Talk to your current employer, explain the situation and see what they're willing to do," I replied.

He came back to me a few days later and told me that his current employer was ready to nearly match the offer in order to keep him. The decision was in his hands, and he had leverage. As I walked him through the decision, we considered two things. First off, we had to consider the economy. This was at a time where we were getting deeper into a period of economic uncertainty where inflation, the overall economy and the employment trends were becoming more challenging each day. Second, he was in a stable, well-paying job where he was well-treated, and the culture fit his own beliefs. On top of that, he was the only one capable of performing his specific tasks at his current job.

On the other hand, at his new job he would have been one of a larger department and the newest employee. I told him that he would probably be the first to get terminated if the economy slumps.

His commitment to this company and his loyalty were put to the test. The thing is that in business, it is not enough simply to have the coolest headquarters, the trendiest product, or the latest technology. Leading a business requires having compassion and empathy. When leaders take the time to understand and empathize with the needs of their employees, then they go full circle. This is something my son valued the most. With that, he decided to stay at his existing company and to continue his professional growth with them.

When we lead with compassion and empathy, our employees will respond in kind, offering us their full commitment and loyalty. Without this level of engagement from our team members, it will be difficult for us to achieve our goals and realize our vision for the company. By approaching our employees with understanding and respect, we help them feel valued and appreciated.

This builds strong bonds of loyalty that become difficult to break. It establishes a sense of support needed to tackle challenging projects and overcome obstacles along the way.

Furthermore, when we seek success through integrity and authenticity rather than simply reward or status quo, our employees recognize our leadership as valuable and worthy of their time and effort.

If on the contrary a good employee feels disrespected or mistreated at work, it can be incredibly damaging to the overall success of a company. There's a good chance the employee won't even stick around to try and make it work. It's especially true in the 2020's and beyond. The pandemic brought forth a The Great Resignation that was created by the realization that life is short. People don't want to stick around in a job they don't like with people they don't like, the latter being most important. A job can be boring or mundane, but if the team likes each other, it makes the work fun. As a leader, it's your role to create an environment where people feel valued, trusted, and empowered.

It's up to you to lead the people, not necessarily lead the business. If your head is too deep in the sand to realize this truth, you will inevitably lose your top talent. Not only does losing good employees use up valuable time and resources as you search for replacements or new hires, but it also causes setbacks and reduces productivity in the meantime. Treating your employees well is ultimately much less expensive and difficult than dealing with the negative consequences of a bad work environment. By prioritizing workplace respect and creating a positive working culture from the start, companies can set themselves up for more consistent success over the long term.

Empathy and flexibility are key components of successful leadership, so always strive to put yourself in the shoes of your team members and find ways to best meet their needs to show them that they matter. And, remember – when you put your team first, they will put your company first. When the whole team puts the company first, that's how your company will win.

Chapter 6
STAY MISSION DRIVEN

I f you breathe and own or lead a business, you want to grow year over year.

You want to drive profits and exceed benchmarks. There are a few ways to do it, but some will come back to bite you if you pick the wrong path.

In the early '90s, when we started Four Star Distribution, the proud parent of brands such as Special Blend, Foursquare Outerwear, Forum Snowboards, Jeenyus and C1RCA, we faced a choice. We could have either taken shortcuts to boost sales and profits quickly, or we could have stayed true to our values. It's tempting when the option of high growth is vibrant. *What entrepreneur doesn't want high growth, quickly?*

But, that's the trap.

If you choose to cut corners, it's as if you are inflating a balloon at hyperspeed, unable to sense when it's about to pop. Sure, it can work in the short term, but it will never be conducive to the longevity of your brand. Shortcuts are short term, and let's face it, you're here for the long haul.

SOME OF OUR CORE VALUES INCLUDED

Investment in development and testing of new products and product categories

–

Best possible quality production of our products

–

Invest heavily into the team of professional athletes

–

Invest heavily into the creation of snowboarding and skateboarding movies and premiers

–

Invest heavily into marketing of our professional team

–

Carefully consider distribution channels in the early years, we did not sell to chain stores and certainly not to big box stores. We also carefully vetted foreign distributors to avoid gray market selling

–

Work closely with our factories which were located all across the world to ensure highest quality, fair prices, on time delivery, and fair labor practices

Throughout our journey, we chose to stay true to our values. Sure, we didn't grow as fast. It was harder in the short term, but it paid off in the long run. We grew steadily with a solid foundation beneath our feet. That foundation made it hard for us to fall. Not only were our brands seen as genuine, but we were also valued more highly than companies who had taken the easier route. By staying true to our values, we were able to build a strong customer base that would continue to support us for years to come. It was a legacy play. It was the long game. And, it paid off with higher dividends than what the shortcuts would have given us.

Many challenges we encountered along the way made us doubt if we were doing the right thing, but we trusted our belief that true success would come from staying true to who we were and what we believed in. Success goes far beyond profits. By creating a brand and a company foundation focused on values and principles, you'll create a more fulfilling work experience for yourself and your team. This inherently leads to a more cohesive and productive workplace.

Great leadership stems from just that. It's the first chain in the reaction of your team. When your team sees your decisions are rooted in values, ethics, and purpose, they follow suit. When they see leaders putting people and purpose over profits, their commitment to the cause grows. On the other hand, when decisions are rooted in profits and money *only*, the psychological connection to the company's purpose dwindles in the eyes of employees. When leaders put money and profits over their people, both employees internal to the company and customers external to the company, detach. Do this enough, and the bond your employees have with you and with your company will be compromised. This can come in the form of cutting corners in the quality of production and service, in underpaying employees to save a few bucks, and at times, even layoffs.

I say this with one thing in mind — if you never think about profits, you won't win. We need to be mindful of our margins without question, and we should actively look for ways to drive efficiency in the name of savings. So long as those decisions are purely rooted in purpose and ethics, all the pieces will fall where they should. Be intentional about keeping your decisions rooted in the mission of the company. Lead with the company's values at the forefront, and everything else will click into place even when you're looking for ways to cut costs.

Our snowboard and skateboard products were trendy. We had already established the brands, we already had loyal customers. We could have easily sacrificed the quality of our product to cut costs and bulk up our product margins and gotten away with it. We could have lowered our standards to compete with more established companies in domestic and international markets. However, we knew that compromising on quality and authenticity would ultimately limit us. It would harm our brand in the long run.

Instead, we focused on creating a unique product that represented our values and upheld high standards of production. In the meanwhile, other brands that did, in fact, lower their standards and compromise their integrity by going for quick sales saw temporary success. As we watched them, we saw their immediate success and growth, followed by the long-term loss of business. The decision to take shortcuts to the finish line is light on the tongue and heavy on the brand. That weight can crumble the brand to a point of no return.

Take TOMS, for instance. TOMS launched in 2006 after its founder, Blake Mycoskie participated in a shoe drive while on vacation in Argentina. When deciding what was going to be the business' main driving factor, Blake pioneered the One for One® model, which aims to give away a pair of shoes for every pair sold in support of health, education and community development programs. The model was commonly known as TOMS Sell a Shoe, Give a Shoe. By 2013, TOMS was reportedly making 250 million dollars in sales[5] a year and one year later, the company was valued at 625 million dollars. By 2020, they had given over 100,000,000 pairs of shoes and had positively impacted the same amount of lives. How exactly has this been possible when TOMS is giving away products? Simple. Because customers pay for their pair as well as for the donated one, and a bit more. A pair of shoes costs TOMS around $9[6],

5   Business Insider | Irene Anna Kim | https://www.businessinsider.com/rise-and-fall-of-toms-shoes-blake-mycoskie-bain-capital-2020-3

6   Toms Shoes Business Model | One-For-One Model Explained https://www.feedough.com/one-for-one-forerunner-toms-shoes-business-model/

but they are sold for anywhere from $22 to $160. Some accessories, like their sunglasses line, sell for as high as $229 a pair. You can do the math.

In 2021, TOMS evolved the one-for-one model into their "1/3 of Profits for Grassroots Good" giving model, to "provide greater flexibility to evolve philanthropic efforts as communities' needs change." The focus of this new model is investing in three key areas the brand believes lays the groundwork for equity in the communities it supports: boosting mental health, increasing access to opportunity, and ending gun violence. While different from the one-for-one model, the concept of this giving model is also pretty straightforward, TOMS will invest one-third of profits for grassroots good, including cash grants and partnerships with community organizations, to drive sustainable change in marginalized communities including Black, Indigenous and People of Color, LGBTQ+ and Women & Girls. In 2021, TOMS supported[7] over 40 organizations with $2,001,022 in grants, positively impacting over 427,000 lives.

You don't have to be a charitable organization to see the same results as a company like TOMS. Any leader and any company can garner a similar impact so long as their mission is strong and they stand true to it like glue. This will allow for better decision-making, as it provides a clear North Star to guide all actions and strategies. Additionally, it can give a

---

7   TOMS IMPACT REPORT 2021| https://www.toms.com/us/impact/report.html

competitive advantage in the marketplace by differentiating the company from competitors. But that's not all, let's look at some other valuable benefits:

Attracting Top Talent

When mission and purpose ignite the flames of our leadership style and our great company brand, we will naturally start reaping the benefits. We will find that we are attracting the right people to our company—from all angles. And what's our business if not the people that make it? From employees to partners to customers, the people involved with the brand are what determines success for our organization.

Many job seekers today are searching for more than just a salary; they're looking for purpose and alignment with the values of their company. Being a mission-driven leader and allowing your employees to join you on the journey helps them feel more fulfillment and satisfaction in their work, because they know their efforts contribute to something bigger than just profits. By setting a clear vision and living out your core values, you show your employees and potential candidates that your organization is focused on making positive change in the world. They will be more motivated and engaged in their work, leading to higher retention rates and overall satisfaction within the company. Being a mission-driven leader also helps create a sense of unity within the company, as all employees are working towards a common goal, and this can be a major advantage in attracting and retaining top talent.

Attracting Loyal Customers

Customers are also drawn to businesses that stand for something, creating more loyalty and potentially attracting new customers who share similar values. They know your brand's mission defines why your company exists, guiding all of your decisions and actions. And this clear focus can have a powerful impact on attracting and retaining them. When customers feel like they share your company's mission, they become passionate brand advocates, spreading the word about your company to their friends and family.

Additionally, customers are increasingly looking for companies that align with their personal values with which they can create an emotional connection. And guess where does that lead to? Yes, it leads to long-term loyalty and growth for your business. It may sound cheesy, but it's true that customers want to support businesses with meaningful values and a sense of contribution to society. In fact, recent studies[8] show that 79% of consumers prefer to purchase products from a brand that operates with a social purpose and 42% of people would even pay extra for products and services from companies committed to positive social and environmental impact. These mission-driven individuals will not only continue to support your brand, but they'll help create a ripple effect of positive impact on both your business and the world at large.

---

8   The Mission-Driven Brand Advantage https://medium.com/high-alpha/the-mission-driven-brand-advantage-fe5329102741

Attracting Strategic Partners

The mission-driven mindset can also be extremely attractive to potential partners who share your values and want to work towards common goals. These strategic partners can provide valuable resources and expertise to help your company grow and succeed. When they align themselves with an organization that has a strong sense of purpose and a passion for making positive change, it shows that their investment in the partnership will have greater impact and make them feel good about where they are putting their resources.

These strong strategic partnerships will also have a positive effect on employee and customer retention, as they see you committing to working with solid and trustable partners. So yes, being a mission-driven leader may seem like an intangible quality - but it has real and tangible results in terms of bringing together the right team to propel your business forward. And isn't that what true leadership is all about? Building a strong foundation for growth and making lasting change at the same time. It's a win-win situation for everyone involved.

In the early days of building our brands at Four Star, we also saw value in aligning ourselves with respected athletes and professionals in our industry. We did it not only for their support and endorsement of our products but also for the opportunity to expand our reach and gain visibility within the market. In a time before the internet boom and online advertising, establishing these partnerships helped us spread the word about our brand and establish a strong presence. Looking back, it's amazing to see how far we went thanks to the power of these partnerships. My team and I will always value the connections and relationships we have had with those who believed in our brands and what they stood for.

At Four Star Distribution, we were able to leverage the trust and quality of our brands to earn media coverage in magazines and other publications. Yes, we did invest in targeted advertising campaigns, but our excellent products and reputation helped attract attention from journalists covering the industry. We were able to secure front-cover stories and feature articles, providing valuable exposure for our brand at no additional cost. It even led us to try more innovative ways to spread the word and promote our brands. After careful evaluation and research, we partnered with the talented cinematographer Mike McEntire of Mack Dawg Productions, to create snowboard films with our professional athletes. The results were breathtaking and helped us position our brands as leaders in the industry.

If we cheated our mission of providing high quality products to our customers, and instead cut corners and made decisions rooted in anything other than that mission, we wouldn't have been able to form any of those partnerships. We wouldn't have been able to attract the talent and the expertise to help us continue growing. And most importantly, we wouldn't have attracted the customers that fueled our growth. Quality was ingrained as a part of our story, and it grew to become the foundation of our success.

A strong reputation and excellent products are just as valuable as paid advertising. It can pay tenfold what a television ad would pay, and it was an organic form of marketing that sparked word of mouth referrals from customer to customer. Quality was to be woven into every aspect of our business. What is woven into your business? If you have similar standards in keeping happy and sticky customers, happy and sticky employees, and happy and sticky partners, then quality is true to your story as well.

It starts with the team members you hire and carries through to every stage of the production process, from raw materials selection to final inspections before shipping. Even when it comes to sales and distribution, make sure to partner with companies and retailers who share the same commitment to delivering exceptional products and experiences to customers. In my experience, this focus on quality in all facets of the business leads not only to satisfied customers, but will also increase profitability and long-term success. It will be tempting to cut corners or settle for less than stellar results to save time or money. But in the long run, investing in quality pays off.

There are countless small businesses and startups out there, all competing for the attention and patronage of customers. There are two things that set successful entrepreneurs and winning leaders apart from those who struggle or fail — **passion and purpose.** If you aren't truly invested in your business and brand, it will show in every aspect of your operations. Your lack of enthusiasm may turn customers away and make it difficult to maintain motivation in the face of challenges. Your lack of buy-in will trickle down to your greater team, and it will be recognized by your competitors.

Rather, a deep passion and a strong purpose are hard to miss. They can drive innovation, attract loyal customers, and keep you motivated through tough times. Without passion, it will be an uphill battle to find success. Without purpose, every challenge will feel like a mountain to climb, and every breakthrough will lack the excitement and drive to propel you forward. As a great leader, your passion and purpose will translate into everything from your marketing efforts to your customer service. Instead, believe in what you are offering to the world and focus your energy on a business that ignites your passions and inspires dedication – that is the key to achieving lasting success. That is the key to being a leader of impact and change.

Ultimately, fulfilling our potential as a leader and as a business requires more than just matching the success of others. Rather, it means staying true to who we are and what we believe in. As the old saying goes, slow and steady wins the race. Don't take your eyes off your mission, no matter how big you get or how far you go. The moment you do, you'll risk it all.

Exercise:

What is your company mission?

_____

_____

_____

_____

What is your personal mission in life?

_____

_____

_____

_____

Chapter 7
EMBRACE SETBACKS

N othing in life comes easy. Anything worth pursuing in this lifetime will inevitably come with its own challenges. It doesn't matter if it's in your professional or personal life, this truth rings loudly across all your initiatives at play — whether it be to build an unbreakable bond with your spouse or gain more market share in your industry. It will be challenging to achieve your goals. If it's not, you haven't set the right goals. The key is that your goals are aligned with your greater purpose and mission at hand. When you operate out of that mindset, you'll welcome the hard. You'll embrace the setbacks, and you'll indulge in the challenges.

It will be challenging to achieve your goals. If it's not, you haven't set the right goals.

Great business leaders are able to lead their teams through tough times with positivity and determination, never losing sight of their passion for the company and its mission. They understand that hitting roadblocks is part of the journey. More importantly, they do not stop because the road is blocked, they find a way around it. They see it as an opportunity for growth. It's how a leader handles these obstacles that ultimately determines their success.

In my own experience as a business owner, I've faced difficulties. Through each difficulty, I always maintained a positive mindset and kept pushing forward. In the end, those challenges have only made me stronger and more prepared for whatever may come my way. In the heat of each challenge, it would have been easy to throw in the towel or give up. But if I did, I wouldn't have made it to where I did. Success is not about avoiding failure, but about how to persevere through setbacks. When you master the art of learning from a failure and using that to find a new path forward, that is when a leader will truly win.

We all think we know this, we've heard it a million times— *Failure is the prerequisite to success.* But, for some reason, the moment we are face to face with a challenge or failure, this mindset deflates. It's easy to let emotions like fear, doubt, and anxiety sway our mindset when faced with adversity. That's why it's important to keep tactics in your back pocket that will help you stay level headed and cognizant of those emotions that could cloud your perspective in stressful times.

One tactic to help you stay in the race even when you trip on a hurdle is to remember your mission. Remind yourself of why you started this journey in the first place. What was your initial passion and drive for this project, for this business? What sparked your interest and ignited your fire? The key here isn't to just think about it or let it roll off your tongue and be done with it. When you ask yourself these questions, you need to dig deep into what your mission is, and dig deeper into why your mission is what it is. Why are you doing this? Chances are, it's bigger than you.

When it's bigger than you, nothing can stop you. We can only do big things when we believe in big things. That's the power of belief, and that belief is and should always be the root of your mission and purpose. Without that foundation, you're just as likely to tumble as a house of cardboard in a windstorm.

When I'm faced with a challenge that seems like a deal breaker, I pause. I stop and think about my purpose as a human being, and the purpose of my work. What is the mission of my business? This helps me to reconnect with my core goals and focus on what truly matters. Additionally, networking with other like-minded individuals helps to keep me energized and inspired. Hearing about the successes and obstacles faced by others reminds me that I am not alone in this journey, and their experiences often open up new possibilities for overcoming my own challenges.

Oftentimes, failure can occur after a long period of success. Take Steve Jobs, for example. He achieved great success at a young age only to find himself unemployed. He thought he was at the top of his game, but the Board of Directors had something else in mind. Jobs was fired from his own company, but he didn't let that setback stop him. He took it as motivation. He treated this as an opportunity to think creatively rather than something negative like many people might expect it would be in their situation. The door at Apple closed, but that led him to start other amazing organizations such as NeXT, a software company, and Pixar, a company that produces animated films like Finding Nemo.[9]

In situations like this it's easy to feel overwhelmed and want to give up. But, it's in those tough moments that true leaders shine. When one door closes, five doors open. The winners in this world stay vigilant to make sure their focus stays on the doors opening rather than the ones that just closed. Each problem you'll face as a leader, no matter its magnitude, presents an opportunity for growth. It presents opportunities that can often lead to unexpected success.

Take, for example, a problem we encountered when producing the Forum bindings. These bindings were produced in a factory in Italy. Due to the fact that a large part of Italy took vacation in the month of August and many factories, including the one producing our bindings, they ran on a strict production schedule to hit our July deadline. We had to be completed with production before the whole country shut down. If production

---

9   https://www.growthink.com/content/7-entrepreneurs-whose-perseverance-will-inspire-you

was not completed by July, we would have to wait until September to complete production and ship the bindings from the factory. This usually caused unacceptable delays for our customers, air shipments instead of sea shipments, increased freight costs, cancellation of orders due to the delay and many other problems.

In this case, the production was completed on time and we started to ship from the factory in July - the hottest month. One of our longest shipping routes was from Italy to Japan. The bindings were boxed and loaded into containers and put on a ship that would sail for weeks via the Suez Canal, the Indian Ocean and the South China Sea to deliver the products to Japan. After our distributor in Japan received and inspected the shipment, I received a message with pictures showing the rubber logo labels which were attached to the bindings during production detached inside the boxes. Of course, we only found out at the least convenient moment — when the containers were opened in Japan.

Mind you that we had no reason to believe something like this would happen, we had shipped products from that same factory at the same time of year to the same destination with no issues in previous years. So now the question was, what went wrong during the production process? After due research with the factory team, we found out that production took place just fine but that the container heating up to unusual levels was the problem. Dealing with this roadblock required some unconventional thinking and outside-the-box problem solving but being able to successfully navigate the obstacles made all the difference in the success of our business.

I could have easily stayed behind and had members of my team deal with the situation, but I joined them and helped. I jumped in without hesitation because it's a leader's responsibility to take initiative and find solutions that drive the company forward. It can be tempting to shy away from difficult tasks and leave them for someone else to handle. However, when you step up and tackle problems head-on, you not only demonstrate your ability as a leader but also set an example for your team. You must roll up your sleeves and work tirelessly. You must embrace the challenge, go in and solve it like the fearless leader you are.

Many other things have happened, almost as if my problem-solving skills were being put to the test to prove I had what was needed to make our company succeed. In 1999, we came out with the C1RCA CM901 skate shoes, the most expensive skateboard sneaker in history, designed by the professional skateboarder and entrepreneur Chad Muska. This model was a limited edition produced in South Korea and had a retail price tag of $ 99 in the United States. We've always prided ourselves on our high quality, but this shoe was so special that it needed to be more than perfect. We took all the necessary time to find the perfect tools and materials, and we tested them extensively until we were happy with the results. All this only to find out later that the factory decided to substitute one of the materials for a cheaper, lower-quality version. This caused the material in the toe area to break with the extensive movement and flexibility that skateboarding requires.

We also faced major inventory and logistics issues caused primarily by our supply chain solution partner at the time. This partner would manage our third-party logistics in the United States, so we would ship all of our products to their warehouse, and they would fulfill the orders from our customers. Now, snowboards come in different sizes and models, and so does clothing, right? Well, the warehouse team decided they would fulfill the orders with just the first product at hand, regardless of the model and size requested, so hundreds of our clients ended up receiving the wrong item. Imagine the number of complaints, returns, inventory, and shipping issues this caused. It was a logistical and customer relations nightmare. After other efforts to improve the situation, such as enhanced training, failed, we ended up investing in renting our own warehouse and hiring our own crew to do the job. It was a decision that required a lot of time, hand power, capital and effort.

As an entrepreneur, stepping out of my comfort zone and embracing uncertainty has led me to unexpected successes and even opened new doors for my business. As time went on, I realized that not doing it would hold me back from reaching my full potential and achieving true success. Yes, sometimes it can feel like every decision carries weight and could potentially lead to disastrous consequences. Taking those bold leaps can be scary. But the rewards will always outweigh any temporary discomfort or fear of failure. And while it is natural to feel stressed and uncertain in the face of obstacles, I have learned that these challenges also provide opportunities for growth and improvement. The key is to approach them proactively instead of letting them consume you with negativity.

It was early November 2003 when I was sitting at the Incheon Airport in Seoul, changing planes from Busan to LAX. It had been a very busy trip, and I was taking time to catch up on emails to our teams in the various offices as well as to some of our suppliers, thanking them for their hospitality. That's when my phone beeped, indicating that I had a voicemail.

As I listened to the message, a sense of surprise overcame me. The message was from a gentleman at E&Y in New York City stating that he would like to speak with me about one of his clients who is interested in purchasing some of our brands. Due to the time difference, I could not call him back prior to take off. Needless to say, the curiosity festered the entire flight home.

Once I was back in the US I called the gentleman from E&Y, and we went through the usual song and dance. When I asked who the client was, he told me he was not at liberty to disclose. We agreed that we would sign an NDA and then the name of the client would be disclosed. Of course, due to the size of the snowboarding industry and the location of the E&Y office, I had to assume Burton was their client. This was confirmed once we signed the NDA. I was invited, along with our COO, to attend an initial meeting with Burton at the E&Y offices in New York City.

We made the meeting, spent a day together with the Burton folks, and shortly thereafter, Burton sent a letter of intent. By this time, it's January 2004 — selling season for the industry. We attended tradeshows in the US, Canada, and Europe and were very busy. We had to finish the selling season and place purchase orders with suppliers, all while preparing reports for Burton. It wasn't until the end of March that things started to slow down. By that point, communications had broken down and didn't take off again until I called Burton's CEO, LP, spoke with him on the phone, and arranged a lunch meeting at Ciao Pasta in San Juan Capistrano. After all, the first meeting was in NYC and I thought it was appropriate for the second meeting to be in our backyard. This time, it was only LP and I meeting over lunch, and we negotiated the deal right then and there. The sale of our snow brands to Burton — aka Project Carve — closed in early August 2004.

If I didn't reach out to LP, this deal might not have happened. If I had given up on any one of the setbacks that fell on my lap along this journey, our company wouldn't have made it to the point of being acquired. If I let the inevitable challenges of leadership and entrepreneurship stop me, I wouldn't have won.

It takes courage to tackle problems head-on, there may be hard decisions to make or uncomfortable conversations to have, but by tackling the issue immediately, we can mitigate its impact. After all, the longer you wait, the bigger and more damaging the problem becomes. Instead of succumbing to despair, use the problem as an opportunity to show your creativity and resourcefulness by finding a solution. And once you do find that solution, don't just pat yourself on the back and move on – use the experience as a learning lesson because it can not only lead to solutions that not only resolve the issue at hand but also prevent similar problems from happening again in the future. As the saying goes, "when the going gets tough, the tough gets going."

Grit and determination are crucial for any successful leader. Next time you encounter a roadblock, remember that it's not about avoiding failure but about how you choose to bounce back from it that makes all the difference. Be passionate, stay motivated, keep learning, and most importantly, never give up. Embrace the struggle and trust yourself to find the solution. That's what being a true leader is all about. It's easy to succumb to frustration and discouragement in these moments, but the true mark of a successful leader is one who knows how to remain passionate and motivated in the face of adversity.

Chapter 8
THE WINNER'S TRAP

*WARNING: IT CAN BE DEBILITATING

The winner's trap — it's debilitating.

Far too many leaders and high performers fall into this trap, and it's something that you need to be aware of if you want to avoid it. Once we get to a certain point in our lives, it can be easy to fall into the trap of thinking we know everything. It's easy to take your foot off the gas pedal once you reach certain goals and have little left to discover what you initially set out to do. To build on that dulled mindset that naturally occurs for many, it also is reinforced. You see, when we reach that point, we are often surrounded by people who constantly agree with us and reinforce our beliefs. Very few challenge our ideas and processes. Your mindset trips you into the trap, and the social reinforcement seals the trap door.

This very trap is what keeps the good from being great. It's what casts a shadow on the desire to explore, create, innovate, and compete with yesterday's self. For anyone to grow in any aspect of life, they need a new perspective that challenges the existing perspective. For that new perspective to have any impact, it requires an open mind and a willingness to learn from those around us. The greatest leaders are the leaders who consistently seek out new perspectives and heightened awareness.

As a matter of fact, our level of success or experience has nothing to do with the limits we place on ourselves. No matter how far we have risen, there will always be room for improvement and new ideas. There will always be room to grow more empathetic, more in tune with others, and more aligned with our true purpose and potential. If you think about it, personal growth comes either through adversity or through intention. When we go through a challenge, we innately learn from it and become better equipped. But, those who intentionally seek personal growth in their day to day are the ones who show up to the challenge having cultivated a mindset that will help them rise above whatever lies before them. Beyond that, those who intentionally seek personal growth are the ones who will leave the greatest impact in this world.

Continuously seeking out new ideas and keeping an open mind is crucial if you want to win the race. This doesn't mean discarding our own values and beliefs; rather, it means being open to alternative perspectives and experiences. From reading books, attending seminars, and hiring a coach, there are various avenues that you can pursue when it comes to personal growth. One of the most important of the bunch, however, is mentorship. In fact, successful leaders often credit mentors as playing a key role in their development. The right mentor offers valuable insight and guidance that will point you in the right direction as a leader and as a business.

You're probably thinking - I know. And you probably do. But how many mentors do you have, if any? Tony Grebmeier, the author of *Power of Fulfillment* and CEO of *ShipOffers* once said, "If you don't have 5 or more mentors in your life, you don't have enough." That's right — 5 or more. Not just one. The reason for that is because there is no one person who can guide you to maximize every aspect of your life. Each person has their own superpower, and when you find a mentor, you should bring them into your life for that specific superpower. For example, Steve Jobs mentored Mark Zuckerberg around how he could manage and develop Facebook and the ins and outs of entrepreneurship.[10] Steve was mentoring Mark in one thing – starting and running a technology company. He wasn't talking to Mark about how to be a good dad or a good husband. He wasn't guiding Mark in how to manage his finances. He wasn't teaching Mark how to keep up with his health and wellness.

---

10   https://www.pushfar.com/article/15-famous-mentoring-relationships/

Find the right mentor for the right segment of your life. Do you need help in your marriage? Then find a couple who you aspire to be like, who has cultivated a loving and supportive relationship. Do you need help with your finances? Then hire a financial advisor who can guide you. Life is not meant to be done alone, and that's especially true in business.

Driving a business to success is not a one man show. Today's business climate is so competitive that to thrive, both you and your team must continuously strive for personal and professional growth. This strengthens the entire team and organization, helps you stay current with industry trends and sharpens everyone's skill sets. With that inherently comes increased productivity and natural differentiation between you and your competitors. It's one thing if you do the work to reach your highest self, but if your team does the work, then you all are unstoppable. Investing in the development of our teammates helps to foster a positive work culture and sets the foundation for future success. It's a recipe for fulfillment, and it's one of the keys to winning.

Now, all the courses, books, and coaching in the world won't get you far if you lack the most important factor we keep coming back to across all ten tactics we're discussing in this book. It all goes back to one thing: *belief*. If you don't believe in yourself, you're in trouble. You will hit a wall at some point and you'll fall. Being a successful leader often means making tough decisions, facing challenges head on, and inspiring those around you to do the same. To do that effectively, you must embody self-belief. This doesn't mean pretending that you never make mistakes, or always showing up at a level ten to prove yourself to your team or even to yourself. It means having the confidence in your skills and capabilities to navigate any difficult situation.

Believing in yourself makes all the difference. With a strong belief in yourself, your purpose, and your team, you not only open the door to decisive decision making, but you will be able to make a decision and *stand by it* without regret or remorse. Even in the face of adversity, you will not waver.

Instead of allowing your doubts to hinder you, trust in your own skills and capabilities. Lead with faith and believe in your own abilities to succeed, even if you have to fake it until you make it. The more you squash doubtful thoughts right as they arise, the stronger your mindset will become. Work on strengthening your belief in yourself, and do what you need to do to show yourself you can be what you envision yourself to be at the end of the race — a winner.

This is something I've found to be true since I was young. In fact, if it wasn't for self-belief, I wouldn't have proved to myself and everyone around me that I had what was needed to succeed in school. When I was in 9th grade, I decided I wanted to attend high school. In order to do that, I had to take the entrance exam to the Cantonal School, the only high school in Frauenfeld, the Capital city of our canton. Keep in mind, I was in Switzerland and entrance exams from 6th grade to secondary school and from 9th grade to high school were normal prerequisites. To my surprise, one of my 9th grade teachers thought I was reaching for an impossible goal. He told my parents that allowing me to try would be a waste of everyone's time, because I would never pass the entrance exam. In moments like those when you must decide if you let criticism affect you or help you, it can be easy to let negative criticism bring us down. It's honestly hard not to leave feeling helpless and defeated. It's important to remember that criticism is just someone else's opinion and doesn't determine our self-worth. Instead of allowing it to bring us down, we can use it as motivation to improve ourselves and prove the critics wrong. Use it as fuel.

If the critique is constructive, it can provide valuable insight and help us identify where we may need improvement. If the critique is not particularly helpful or fair, we can still use it as a reason to work harder and continually strive for personal growth. Ultimately the only approval that matters is your own. Reflect on yourself and use any valuable insights as fuel for further growth. In my case, I didn't let negative criticism define me – I turned it into motivation instead.

In every circumstance that we find ourselves subject to another person's opinion, stop and think about the critique objectively. Detach yourself from the emotion it triggers, and:

> **"**
>
> **If someone criticizes you, stop and think about the critique objectively. Detach yourself from the emotion it triggers, and:**
>
> - **Determine whether they have any valid points,**
> - **Use those points as motivation to grow,**
> - **Embrace the challenge of overcoming those doubts.**
>
> **"**

Rather than getting defensive or giving up, I considered the criticism carefully and tried to identify any valid points. Then, I used those points as motivation to learn and improve. I embraced the challenge and worked hard, and it paid off. I passed the entrance exam, and it was an achievement that boosted my self-esteem for a long time.

Even though being accepted to the school was my biggest academic success to date, after spending a semester at Cantonal School, I could tell it was not the place for me. It was just like when you start a new job that you're very excited about and then the culture and values just don't match yours. The spark starts to fade out. I felt like I needed to try something different that would better match my interests and strengths, so I switched to an apprenticeship where I could learn and work simultaneously in agriculture.

And there I learned another lesson. I was 16 years old when I started looking for an apprenticeship. The one I selected included one year of practical experience on a farm plus two years on a hybrid model that combined education and practical experience at the Agriculture School. For the year of practical experience, I chose the farmer I wanted to work with, called and asked for an appointment - I had to explain the reason for my visit. The farmer agreed to see me and interview me for the job. By the end of the interview, the farmer asked me how much I wanted to earn. I said I did not know and he didn't hesitate to reply that, in that case, he would not pay me a dime. Imagine my shock and disappointment. But I was not willing to give up the opportunity and thought about it for a minute. I knew that some of my friends had earned 350 Swiss Francs per month in their first year of apprenticeship, so I asked the farmer for 500 Swiss Francs per month, plus room and board. It seemed reasonable to me considering that my job would be from 4am - until 8pm, with some weekend days off. To my surprise, the farmer agreed and I was able to secure a job and the start of my apprenticeship. Long story short, the lesson here is - always be prepared and know all the facts you need to know to make informed decisions.

I kept an open mind and soon understood that I didn't need to take the common route where you go to a traditional school, then get a degree from a university and finally get a job. Instead, I could create my own journey and make sure my education focused on my own interests, skills and abilities rather than a pre-made curriculum that blanketed all students of all backgrounds. While it can be tempting to try to fit into a prescribed mold of success, chasing after traditional measures is like trying to live up to others' expectations. Then, you just find yourself right back into the hot seat of others' opinions and ideas over your own.

If that's something that resonates with you, it's possible that you've also wanted to create your own development path. I say, go for it. Focus on the areas where you shine and have the opportunity to reach your full potential. This doesn't mean that you should ignore areas in need of improvement or avoid challenging yourself, but you can prioritize learning and growth in areas aligned with your passions. You'll soon find that by focusing on what truly inspires and energizes you, you will likely find that professional success naturally follows.

One of the stops I made on my journey to personal and professional development was to challenge myself to fix past issues that I had been dragging on. When my wife once came home completely refreshed and renewed after experiencing the seminar *Daybreak: A Personal Growth Experience*, I went and signed up to try it out for myself and see if I could achieve excellent results as well. It turned out to be one of the best decisions I've made.

During the seminar, I was able to unlock and heal many wounds, and that took a lot of weight off my shoulders. It made me realize that we all have things in our past that weigh heavily on us, and it can be hard to acknowledge and heal from these experiences. Taking the time to process and work through painful memories allows us to let go and move forward with our lives. It opens up space for personal growth in relationships, career, and overall wellbeing and while it can be a difficult and challenging process, it can also be incredibly freeing and empowering.

If you want to have a thriving business, be a successful leader and inspire and motivate your team, the best place to start is by committing to personal and professional growth yourself. So often, we get caught up in our day-to-day tasks and lose sight of our goals and aspirations. By making a conscious effort to improve yourself, you not only set a positive example for your team but you also create opportunities for collaboration and growth for others.

Challenge yourself to try new things, confront personal weaknesses, and build healthier relationships with those around you. Your team will not only see the benefits in your own performance, but they'll also feel inspired to do the same for themselves. If you lead by example and pave the way for a culture of continuous personal and professional development within your team, the results will speak for themselves in increased productivity and morale. And ultimately, everyone will reap the rewards of becoming better individuals both inside and outside the workplace. After all, this will not only break up the monotony of daily tasks, but also create a more well-rounded and connected team.

One thing is for sure — standing still is not an option. It is not enough to simply stay comfortable with our current skills and knowledge. As leaders, it's our responsibility to continuously seek out new knowledge and skills for ourselves and for our team. It's in our hands to create a positive and productive work environment where everyone is striving for excellence. The world is constantly evolving, and a successful leader must adapt and grow with it. This means being open to feedback, seeking out new perspectives, and constantly expanding your knowledge base. It also involves actively creating an environment where team members feel comfortable voicing their own ideas and experiences, allowing for mutual learning and growth.

Our businesses will only thrive when we surround ourselves with diverse thinkers and continually challenge ourselves to grow and improve. Our level of awareness across different aspects of our lives will only expand as we welcome new ideas and perspectives from trusted mentors and intentional and pointed self-education. Afterall, having a growth mindset not only benefits our work life, but also allows us to bring fresh perspectives and energy into every aspect of life — from our relationships to our health. Embrace opportunities for growth and never stop striving to become a better version of yourself as a leader. The best leaders never stop learning.

Chapter 9
SYNC YOUR PERSONAL AND PROFESSIONAL LIFE

The pandemic was a catalyst for bringing work life balance into the spotlight, but it's been something that has crippled many workers across the globe, particularly in the corporate world, for years. A study that surveyed 1,850 people managers across six countries found that 63 percent of respondents were thinking of quitting their jobs. The reason? Because of a poor work-life balance and/or burnout. In addition to that, 2 in 5 people managers thought about quitting themselves — including 53% of managers in the U.S. and the U.K. [11]

Work-life balance is not just a buzzword — it's about taking control of our own happiness and well-being. But,

---

11   https://www.ukg.com/resources/article/resign-resigned-or-re-sign?rq=1&gt=1

let's be honest. Work life *balance* is tough. You can't be in two places at once, and some seasons of your life will require you to pour into one aspect of your life more than another to reach your goals. Rather than balance, the appropriate pursuit should be toward work-life synergy. When you think of synergy, you think of all sails moving in the same direction, thus, making the ship move faster. But, what does that mean when it comes to your personal and professional life?

It starts with your mission. When you operate based on your life's mission, and more importantly, serve a company that embodies a mission you align with, it's easy to set your emotional, mental, and actionable sails in the same direction as your work. Furthermore, it comes down to being intentional. Work life synergy only comes when you intentionally stay present in each element and intentionally design your days to best fit your *values.*

It's also about committing to making positive changes in our daily routines and creating a fulfilling life that incorporates both work and play. It's crucial for both our personal satisfaction and professional success, especially for those of us in leadership roles where the constant responsibility, stress, and pressure can quickly become overwhelming. However, if we have control over our well-being and make time for those things that bring us joy and fulfillment, we are better able to inspire others and perform at our highest level.

The issue may be that when it comes to work-life synergy, many of us tend to focus on what we're missing out on. Some yearn for more free time, fantasize about taking extended vacations, and even dream of quitting their jobs to pursue a passion project. Others get caught up in the daily grind and prioritize work over everything else. That's when having a balanced approach to both your personal and professional life comes in.

Here are some tactics to incorporate to help you find the synergy you need in order to keep a full cup, even when work gets busy.

Set Boundaries

Setting boundaries is critical in your pursuit to protect your bandwidth and avoid burnout. But, how can you do it without looking like you're not a team player or simply don't want to do something? Try things like:

- Asking for help, whether it's from another leader in the company, your boss, a mentor, or even hiring a consultant.
- Rank and prioritize your to-do list. What projects need to be completed by you (and don't you dare say all of them), and which ones can you delegate to others?
- Focus on communication — Make sure you're crystal clear on other peoples' expectations of you and your expectations of others.
- Take your time when responding to an ask. The next time someone asks something of you, just say "Let

me check my schedule (or bandwidth) and see if I can make it happen." Pause, then respond. Truly think through whether you are able and willing to take on a task, and whether you can do it at full energy or if it will drain you. If it will drain you, be honest and say you're concerned about bandwidth or schedules syncing up.

- Prioritize your values. If you are a parent or have other social and relational obligations, try not to miss them. When you are able to be present in more elements of your life, you will be able to create synergy across the board much easier.

Indulge in Hobbies

- Too many people in the world let their hobbies and favorite activities fall to the wayside because they're too busy. So much to do, so little time — right? Wrong. You decide. Time block your calendar to read, write, sing, hike, garden — whatever it is you like to do — once a week. This, alone, will fill your cup and help you get reenergized.

- Spend more time outside. If the weather is nice, take your hobby outside. Get some sunshine. When you work in an office, it requires that you're intentional about seeing the day of light. As a matter of fact, being outside in green spaces specifically can lower the risk of depression and enables faster psychological stress recovery. Being in nature can restore and strengthen our mental capacities, and help us to increase focus and attention.[12] To supplement your performance at work and in your personal life, just get outside more.

Self Care

- You guessed it — exercise. It doesn't have to be rigorous, it could just be an afternoon walk that you incorporate into your routine. The benefits of exercise are well worth the 30 minutes of discomfort you feel during the work out. You'll not only feel more energized, have more level emotional responses, and feel more confident, you will be happier. The endorphins that come with a heart rate spike have been proven to help improve your mood, help you relax, and lower symptoms of mild depression and anxiety.[13]

- Get more sleep. You should get 7-8 hours of sleep every night in order to maintain stress and feel fully refreshed the next day.

Be Present

- Pause between tasks. Take 5 minutes to close your eyes for a quick meditation after you finish one task and before you move onto the next.

- When you're working on a project, set a timer that outlines 30 minutes to an hour of deep, uninterrupted

---

12   https://www.fs.usda.gov/features/wellness-benefits-great-outdoors#:~:text=There%20are%20many%20mental%20 wellness,capacities%2C%20increasing%20focus%20and%20attention.

13   https://www.mayoclinic.org/healthy-lifestyle/stress-management/in-depth/exercise-and-stress/art-20044469

work. Until that timer is up, don't get up, don't check your phone, just focus on the task at hand.

- When you're in a meeting, be in that meeting. When you're with your family and friends, be with your family and friends. Get off your email, get off your phone, and be present.

- Incorporate the 3-Step Decision process discussed in chapter 3 when making decisions. This requires you to take time and be present in each decision you make, leading you to better decision-making overall.

It's easier said than done. Our lives are in a constant state of flux, making the strife toward work-life synergy a constant struggle. The key is to remember that life is about the journey, not the destination. It's about constantly evaluating our priorities and making choices that align with those values. And just like any belief system, there will be times when we stray from those principles and have to reset and refocus. That's okay. What's important is that we never give up on our goal of achieving harmony in all aspects of our lives. By consistently checking in with ourselves, setting boundaries, and being intentional about our health, wellness, and joy, we can ultimately create a fulfilling and balanced lifestyle.

For me, it works to keep in mind that a successful life means more than just achieving career success. It involves maintaining balance in all areas of life, including relationships, family, personal well-being, and more. This can be a difficult feat to accomplish. I've honestly been at the verge of failure many times, but I have a partner that has been looking out for me for the past 36 years: My wife.

I'm grateful to have her by my side helping me maintain that balance. She is the voice of reason when I start getting too caught up in work, reminding me to prioritize my health and spend quality time with my loved ones. And while she supports my professional pursuits with the same persistence, she pushes me to set aside time for self-care and growth as an individual. Through her guidance and support, I'm able to stay grounded and attend to all facets of my life rather than getting consumed by just one. She truly helps keep the harmony in our home and enables me to lead a fulfilling and well-rounded life.

Whether it's your significant other, your friend, or another family member, it's important to welcome others into your journey. When they share with you that something seems off about you, welcome the feedback. Many times, we have blind-spots that we can't see ourselves but it may be blinding to those who know us well. Keep an open heart and open mind to feedback and make necessary adjustments that will lead to more synergy and balance across all aspects of your life.

Think about achieving work-life balance as an investment in yourself and your overall happiness, not just about being able to juggle responsibilities. Sometimes on purpose, sometimes not, we neglect those non-work-related stops on our life journey, ignoring that they matter just as much as any business meetings or deadlines. When we add balance as an essential component of our personal and professional development, and work hard but also remember to take care of ourselves, when we really make that effort, not only do we protect our mental and physical health, but we also set ourselves up for more productivity, creativity, and success in the long run. If we get to find that harmony, we are more able to approach our work with a refreshed mindset and renewed energy, which also leads to improved mental health and overall happiness.

This is one of the reasons why finding ways to give back has become an integral part of my work-life balance formula. It reminds me that I'm only a part of something larger and adds perspective to my own struggles and challenges. From volunteering to support a local organization to donating time and money to a worthy cause, not only does giving back makes me feel good, as I know that I am contributing to the betterment of my community and the world at large, but it also helps me stay grounded and connected to the bigger picture. It serves as a reminder that as blessed and privileged as I may be in my own life, there are others who are not as fortunate and could use a helping hand. Through giving back, I have found purpose in helping others and discovered new avenues for personal growth and self-improvement. And the fulfillment that comes with making a positive impact on the world around me is immeasurable and unmatched by anything else in my day-to-day life. Realigning my priorities to include giving back has brought significant growth and happiness into my life, and I encourage everyone to incorporate it into their own work-life balance formula because it not only enriches our personal relationships and connects us to our community, but it also brings greater satisfaction to our professional life as well.

Beyond that, it's important to realize that balance and synergy is also a matter of attitude. It's a choice of perspective. If you spend a lot of time going around in circles because something didn't go your way at work, or you're too busy drowning in work-related problems that you could have solved proactively or even turn into opportunities, you will also be too busy to enjoy the rest of your life. When life throws a challenge my way, rather than feeling defeated or giving up right away, I put my positivity cap on and choose to see them as opportunities for growth and learning.

Sure, it's easy to become discouraged when things don't go as planned, it's actually human nature to let our minds slip into a negative perspective when our emotions get involved. But, again, we have to be intentional – intentional about choosing to stay determined and keeping a positive attitude. If we master this skill (yes, it's a skill that you can and need to develop), it will inevitably lead to success in the long run. That should be our north star, because quitting would mean missing out on the chance to reach your full potential and achieve something amazing. Winners never quit.

By constantly pushing forward and finding solutions instead of throwing in the towel, I have learned that adversity makes us stronger and more resilient in the end. It just depends on our mindset. Do we pay victim or victor? Do you throw a pity party and slow down in your trajectory because something at work didn't go as planned? If that's you, I'd be willing to bet that you carry that with you when you go home in the evening. That, then, trickles into how you treat your family, what coping mechanisms you use to deal with stress, and your ability to be present in the other aspects of your life.

> **❝**
>
> **Adversity makes us stronger. It just depends on our mindset.**
>
> **Are you the victim or the victor?**
>
> **❞**

You either need to learn to turn it off when you leave the office and stop thinking about it completely until you're back at your desk, or you need to do a full rehaul of your mindset toward life. Sure, you could let adversity slow you down, or you could keep moving forward, full steam ahead, and roll over whatever stands in your way. You don't quit. You don't question your future when things get hard. You accept that it's part of the deal, and you persevere.

As a leader, it is equally important to remember that success should not come at the cost of the well-being of your team members. We need to prioritize work-life balance for everyone and create a culture where balance is encouraged and not penalized. By valuing and promoting work-life balance in our businesses, our employees will feel confident in taking time for themselves and replenishing their energy. And it only comes for our team if it comes for us.

Leaders set the bar. Remember when you first started your career, and the stigma was that those who show up before and leave after the boss are the ones who get the furthest? Your team still thinks that, or at least the high performers do. If you have no synergy and balance in your professional and personal life, then your team will lack it as well. Many organizations are flawed in thinking that when employees are on the clock for hours at a time, uninterrupted, that productivity finds its own synergy and increases output. Sure, that's true to an extent, but a lack of work life balance will almost always lead to burnout. I will always reach a tipping point where productivity turns into burnout. A group of burnt out employees will produce the opposite of what you're aiming for, and it is only a matter of time.

On the other hand, when your company culture promotes time with family and friends, self care, hobbies, etc. you are cultivating a culture that promotes professional and personal synergy. This can lead to increased job satisfaction, productivity, and overall happiness in both their professional and personal lives. That positive impact will trickle down through your products and services, and help you further differentiate your brand from competitors.

This will not only help us foster a positive work environment, but our teams will also be better equipped to handle any challenges that may arise. The effort begins with us, let's strive to create an environment where our team can come to work feeling refreshed, motivated, and ready to excel.

Finding balance between our professional and personal lives may seem complicated and overwhelming, but we can shift our mindset and focus on the small steps we can take every day towards achieving it. I know that while the work-life balance concept may be easy to talk about, making the effort can be daunting, but actively implementing it in your own life is worth every bit of hard work.

Chapter 10
DON'T EVER QUIT

Many are more in love with the *idea* of being a winner than actually being a winner. It's true, think about it. Who doesn't want to win? However, in today's results-oriented culture, many are only focused on the outcome of something. They only see the praise and the glory, they don't see the struggle that takes place behind the curtains.

True winners know that the struggle and the strife are a piece of the formula to success. Without it, there is no progress. Without challenge, there is no triumph. Without rain, there are no rainbows – in fact, there are no living species left to inhabit this earth. We need rain. We need challenges. Winners embrace that challenge, and they implement the ten factors we've reviewed in this book to help them reach their destination. At no point along their journey do they quit.

True winners know that giving up means settling for less than what they are capable of. Instead, they embrace any setbacks as fuel for their determination to succeed. As I always say, our greatest setbacks often lead to our greatest comebacks. If we choose to see our glass half full and never give up on ourselves, we can become the winners we were always meant to be. Having a balanced life and succeeding isn't about doing everything perfectly; it's about finding a sense of harmony in all aspects of our lives. But in order to do that, we must let go of any negativity and negative patterns holding us back. Rather, we need to embrace our power of positivity as we strive for balance and happiness.

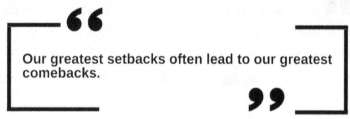

Our greatest setbacks often lead to our greatest comebacks.

Don't be afraid to reflect, prioritize, adjust, and keep striving towards a healthy balance in all aspects of your life journey. Make conscious efforts toward pouring your attention into different areas of your life, and you will find yourself living a more fulfilling and well rounded life. Keep your faith and your mission at the forefront of all your decisions, and let that motivate you to stay standing when times are tough. Embrace challenges, and envision yourself standing on the other side a stronger, more productive and resilient leader. Last, stay nimble and flexible to move as time moves.

The world we live in is fast paced, it changes (what seems like) every day. From evolving technology to progressing cultural and societal norms, the leaders who will win in this century are those who will adapt regularly while still keeping their greater purpose and mission top of mind. It's the leader who will be present on purpose that will reap and sow the most value. It's the leaders who take their time in making decisions, thinking beyond what lies right in front of them in order to stay competitive.

Remember, true leaders become winners because they are not afraid of failure, because they know it is merely a chance to learn and grow. They understand that success does not happen overnight and requires perseverance, dedication, and constant self-improvement. Winners never give up, even in the face of adversity, because they have a strong belief in their own abilities and potential. They are balanced individuals who prioritize wellness in all aspects of their life, allowing them to stay focused on their goals. Above all, they have a positive attitude and outlook. A winner never rests on their laurels – they are always learning, adapting, and looking for new ways to grow.

So, the next time you're facing a decision, a challenge, or an adverse circumstance, ask yourself —

Are you in love with the idea of winning, or are you a winner?

If you're a winner, quitting is not an option. Doubting yourself is not an option. Slowing down is not an option. So long as you live and lead by these 10 key factors, you, too, will be a courageous leader that makes it to the finish line — whatever that finish line may be.

ACKOWLEDGMENTS

Although I'd like to say all these ideas in this book were born in my mind, I can't. I write this book with the utmost gratitude in my heart for all the people in my life who have helped me realize the lessons I've learned throughout my life, both professionally and personally. It's these lessons that I have garnered throughout my life that make this book, and it's all the people and the experiences in my life that have helped me realize these lessons. I hope that these ten keys to leadership help you as much as they have helped me over the years.

From family and friends to partners, employees, and clients, it's truly a privilege to have had each and everyone of you play such a monumental role in my story. Yes, I mean every one of you who has crossed paths with me. I remember you, I am thankful that we have met, worked together, studied together, learned together, traveled together, laughed together and cried together. And to my wife, Sandy — there are not enough words to express my gratitude and appreciation for you standing by my side through all the peaks and valleys of life. I couldn't have done this without you. May God bless you all.

I'd also like to thank you for reading this book. It's merely through the intentional effort put forth by leaders around the world to better themselves that society will better itself. Go strong in the pursuit of your goals, and please stay in touch. I always love hearing about the amazing things my readers do in their work and their lives, and I am always here as a resource for you as you build your legacy.

CONNECT WITH MARKUS BOHI

BohiConsulting.com

—

in LinkedIn.com/in/Markus-Bohi

—

f Facebook.com/MarkusBohiRealEstate

—

Instagram.com/Markus_Bohi

SOURCES

1. Special Collections: Chronology, Social Security Administration, accessed September 2022, https://www.ssa.gov/history/1950.html.

2. Naz Beheshti, "10 Timely Statistics About the Connection Between Employee Engagement and Wellness," Forbes, https://www.forbes.com/sites/nazbeheshti/2019/01/16/10-timely-statistics-about-the-connection-between-employee-engagement-and-wellness/.

3. Naz Beheshti, "10 Timely Statistics About the Connection Between Employee Engagement and Wellness," Forbes, https://www.forbes.com/sites/nazbeheshti/2019/01/16/10-timely-statistics-about-the-connection-between-employee-engagement-and-wellness/.

4. Anjan Pathak, "Importance of Diversity and Inclusion for Business Growth," Entrepreneur, September 10, 2021, https://www.entrepreneur.com/en-in/news-and-

trends/importance-of-diversity-and-inclusion-for-business-growth/.

5. Irene Anna Kim, "How Toms Went from a $625 Million Company to Being Taken Over by Its Creditors," Business Insider, December 27, 2020, https://www.businessinsider.com/rise-and-fall-of-toms-shoes-blake-mycoskie-bain-capital-2020-3.

6. Bharath Sivakumar, "Toms Shoes Business Model | One-For-One Model Explained," Feedough, April 14, 2020, https://www.feedough.com/one-for-one-forerunner-toms-shoes-business-model/.

7. Amy Smith, TOMS Impact Report 2021, https://www.toms.com/us/impact/report.html.

8. Drew Beechler, "The Mission-Driven Brand Advantage," Medium, December 12, 2017, https://medium.com/high-alpha/the-mission-driven-brand-advantage-fe5329102741.

9. Dave Lavinsky, "7 Entrepreneurs Whose Perseverance Will Inspire You," growthink, https://www.growthink.com/content/7-entrepreneurs-whose-perseverance-will-inspire-you.

10. "15 Famous Mentoring Relationships," PUSHfar, https://www.pushfar.com/article/15-famous-mentoring-relationships/.

11. "Resign, Resigned, or Re-Sign?" UKG, https://www.ukg.com/resources/article/resign-resigned-or-re-sign.

12. Andrew Avitt, "The Wellness Benefits of the Great Outdoors," Forest Service, US Department of Agriculture, March 24, 2021, https://www.fs.usda.gov/features/wellness-benefits-great-outdoors.

13. Mayo Clinic Staff, "Exercise and Stress: Get Moving to Manage Stress," https://www.mayoclinic.org/healthy-lifestyle/stress-management/in-depth/exercise-and-stress/art-20044469.

A free ebook edition is available with the purchase of this book.

To claim your free ebook edition:

1. Visit MorganJamesBOGO.com
2. Sign your name CLEARLY in the space
3. Complete the form and submit a photo of the entire copyright page
4. You or your friend can download the ebook to your preferred device

Morgan James BOGO™

A **FREE** ebook edition is available for you or a friend with the purchase of this print book.

CLEARLY SIGN YOUR NAME ABOVE

Instructions to claim your free ebook edition:
1. Visit MorganJamesBOGO.com
2. Sign your name CLEARLY in the space above
3. Complete the form and submit a photo of this entire page
4. You or your friend can download the ebook to your preferred device

Print & Digital Together Forever.

Snap a photo

Free ebook

Read anywhere

Printed in the USA
CPSIA information can be obtained
at www.ICGtesting.com
JSHW022149170924
70033JS00002B/10